A FAMILY'S SECRET

BIPOLAR DISORDER ON TREETOP LANE

Clarence,
May the Lord
bless you throughout
your life!
Carol Horan

CAROL HORAN, M.A., L.M.F.T.

ISBN: 1468150871
ISBN 13: 9781468150872

Library of Congress Control Number: 2012900154
CreateSpace, North Charleston, SC

Author's Note

Names and other identifying characteristics of the persons mentioned in this memoir have been changed, except for the author's. Actual places have been masked. The dates are as accurate as possible and taken from journal writings; others are approximations. My children's memories may be far different from the ones recalled in this memoir. Sadly, they are no less painful.

Dedication

This book is dedicated to my children and grandchildren. One granddaughter may have some dim memories of her biological grandfather when she is an adult. She was four when he died. Another grandson was five months old when his grandfather died on February 9, 2010. And we were blessed with still another grandson on August 17th, 2011. We also have three granddaughters and a grandson on my current husband's side, who though not biologically related to the husband in my story, may benefit from my book.

To all of our grandchildren, I love each of you very much. I hope you can learn from my experiences and hold on to your integrity and values in all of your relationships. Although I sometimes behaved as a victim, I not only survived, but loved life in my later years. Your parents stayed strong through all of what unfolded. I hope that my story reminds you that God loves us all and never leaves our side no matter how difficult the struggle. Paul was a good man who suffered from a brain disorder. He loved his children and we loved him.

I credit my current husband for the book's existence. His persistence and belief in me helped me pursue the dream of creating this book.

Introduction

Our society generally rewards people with a strong work ethic, as I believe it should. And when people begin to work longer hours and focus their lives on their chosen field, they may also increase their benefits. Family and friends may applaud the person with high energy and little need for sleep. We often label ambitious people as *Type A*. They seem driven and relentless in their pursuit of career goals. They often earn the respect and envy of their peers. Many are extremely bright and creative, leading by example. Fortunately, many of these people are able to lead productive and satisfying lives, enjoy the fruits of their labor and earn the privileges of a well-earned retirement and many years as senior citizens. However, for some people, the same patterns of behavior are early warnings of trouble ahead. The non-stop work, lack of sleep and extreme ambition are not signs that all is well. For some, it is an indicator that something else may be happening, possibly a mood or affective disorder. When does a person cross that line between health and illness? This book attempts to show that it is not always easy to discern, especially when one is emotionally connected to a loved one. Many of the symptoms exhibited by my husband coincided with symptoms listed in the DSM IV R for Bipolar I disorder which was available to me at the time of my marriage. It has been updated since then and the newer edition is the Diagnostic Statistical Manuel IV –TR.

For example, when I was twenty-six I was both surprised and happy to see my husband skipping for joy with our baby daughter in his arms. I wasn't worried about her safety; he had no intent of harming her. But now I view that early scene differently. He was probably too euphoric.

Readers concerned about family members and loved ones are encouraged to seek out licensed mental health professionals. They have been trained to identify and treat mental disorders. Some problems may require a diagnosis, therapy and/or medical attention. The challenge is often in getting people to visit the mental health professional and subsequently accepting treatment recommendations from them.

Since one in seventeen Americans lives with a serious mental health disorder, we must find better ways to help those who suffer directly. (Kimball, 2007). According to James Pavle, former director of the Treatment Advocacy Center, "with minimal exception, incarceration has replaced hospitalization for thousands of individuals in every single state."(Torrey, 2010). A fifty state report from the Treatment Advocacy Center and the National Sheriff's Association claims at least sixteen percent of inmates in jails and prisons have a serious mental illness. It also stated that Arizona and Nevada have ten times as many mentally ill in prisons and jails as in hospitals. Outpatient treatment is often unavailable as well. The consequences are alarming and often include homelessness, victimization and death. (Torrey, 2010).

Mental illness has been a neglected public –health issue far too long. We need to provide support for affected families and friends, while also protecting innocent people from being hurt. I urge anyone who has experienced the pain associated with mental disorders to contact your state and local chapters of NAMI (National Alliance on Mental Illness). For over thirty years, NAMI has been reaching out to support individuals and families impacted by mental illness. They advocate for those who are tormented from the disorders and the families who care about them.

Acknowledgments

I'd like to acknowledge my children, the heroes of this story. If I could relive it, I would give it a different ending. But despite what my children endured and the mistakes made by both of their parents, they have matured into caring and responsible adults, who now have their own families and excel in their professions.

I often voiced my appreciation to my father while he lived. I cannot repay him now, but I am grateful for the mutual healing we experienced in his later years. I also thank my step-mother for her sharp intellect, compassion and wisdom, which she continues to offer me.

I'd like to thank one of the ministers of our Lutheran church, who helped our family cope with the emotional tsunami that flooded our lives.

And I'm deeply grateful to my friends in the school district where I worked, as well as my professional colleagues and fellow therapists.

My other special friends in the town where we lived, who offered support when I was unsure of my actions, were invaluable to my family and me. I'd like to thank M.A.T. who read and critiqued my first and sketchy draft manuscript.

And I give special thanks to my editors, Nancy McCurry and Rosa Cays, who believed this manuscript had value. Thanks also to Charles Sanderson for the artwork on the front cover.

In the case of scandal, as in that of robbery, the receiver is always thought as bad as the thief.

— LORD CHESTERFIELD, AKA PHILLIP STRANHOPE, ENGLISH AUTHOR AND STATESMAN (1694-1773)

Be of good courage. Time spent in the difficult is never wasted.

—ANONYMOUS

Good judgment comes from experience, and often experience comes from bad judgment.

—RITA MAE BROWN

Once upon a time a frog was put into a pot of boiling water. This smart frog jumped out immediately to avoid the pain. Another smart frog, however, was put into a comfortable pot of water and didn't notice as the temperature increased one degree at a time. Sadly, this frog boiled to death before noticing how his environment had become deadly.

—ANONYMOUS

Contents

ACT 3

ACT 1

CHAPTER 1

Early Lessons on the Road to Hell

In 1949 when I was three years old I wrapped my arms around my mother's calves as I stood beneath her and said, "Mommy, don't cry."

I followed the request with another: "Daddy, don't make Mommy cry."

I've thought about this vivid memory when I've worked with families as a therapist. Parents have told me their children are too young to remember painful events that occurred to them while very young. I'm sure this belief helps assuage parental guilt over any unpleasantness children have suffered. Although selective memories can be remembered or repressed, it's false to assume children don't remember events because they were too young.

Was this memory the seed that led me to become a marriage and family therapist in adulthood? I knew from an early age my parents' marriage was troubled. It was easy to gather more evidence during my childhood to support this idea. My parents sought me out as a referee when I was very young. Counseling and mediating felt like a natural continuation of a process I had learned to accept as normal throughout my life.

I've spent many hours reflecting on my parents' relationship to better understand the dynamics in my own first marriage. Conversations with my parents when I was a child in our rural Midwestern town hinted at underlying issues, but I could not decode these.

"Mom, can I go swimming with the other kids at the lake?"

"No, honey. You don't want to get polio, do you?" Mom asked.

"What's polio?"

"It's when you get very sick and become paralyzed. You can't move and you may have to live in an iron lung and not walk. You wouldn't want that now, would you?"

"No, Mommy."

"And you might not breathe well afterwards either. Remember how wheezy you get sometimes. You wouldn't want to risk it, would you?" She arched her eyebrows.

"I suppose not," I said. It was years later when I was diagnosed asthmatic. In the early fifties, doctors in our town didn't know about asthma. I was told I had post-nasal drip and so I took nose drops for years. All to no avail.

I don't think my mother was always overprotective, but at times she couldn't seem to help it. Her decisions weren't entirely unwarranted; polio and asthma were real health threats at the time. But as I grew older, I pushed for more activities. I didn't accept externally imposed limitations very well.

I sulked a bit when my little brother was born. I'm not sure why, but I told everyone he was coming from Kansas City. He turned out to be more fun than I thought as he started walking and talking. We fought and competed, but also confided in each other. We shared a room with twin beds when we were young and would talk long after our dad told us to be quiet. We often got a very sharp, verbal reprimand, and in a few cases, a spanking.

I had a long "to do" list as a kid. I wanted to take acrobatics, tap dancing, ballet and piano. My mom explained we had no money for those things, since they would be sending me to "sisters' school," which cost considerable money. So when I was five, I taught myself how to twirl baton, using a pamphlet with illustrations. After practicing awhile, I decided I was ready to open my own school. My mom said I could teach, but not charge. She tried not to be too discouraging.

We put on plays for the mothers in our neighborhood in the summer afternoons. Mothers were at home back then and sought out excuses to get together. The kids in our neighborhood provided it. We collected costumes and involved any child who could walk and talk. Our original scripts provided much laughter.

Right before turning six, I was taken to Monsignor's rectory and the convent to be introduced to the Dominican nuns, who would teach me as soon as I left public kindergarten. I remember feeling shy when introduced to these women in the strange looking black and white clothes called "habits." I thought they looked like penguins, but my parents cautioned me not to mention it.

I learned nuns value clean finger nails and had weekly inspections in first grade. They also valued silence and strict obedience. I sat under the cuckoo clock and was told I had to be able to hear the clock tick when Sister left the room. This was not easy, since the boys were so noisy. We were encouraged to buy saltwater taffy for a dollar a stick. Chocolate, strawberry or vanilla flavors were sold each day, and the money went to help the poor "pagan" babies in Africa. My mother rarely, if ever, gave me money for taffy. Some kids bought it every day. I tried to explain to her I could save more souls if I bought more taffy, but she didn't believe me. She was too concerned about cavities.

At the end of first grade, I received the highest academic average and it was announced from the pulpit in our church. People offered congratulations, and I didn't understand why. When I didn't receive the highest average award after second grade, a mother stopped me as I was leaving church and asked me why I didn't get top honors again.

She asked, "Can't you cut it any more? Not as smart as you thought?"

I had no answer for her. I felt stupid.

I started feeling ashamed about age seven when I started going to confession. I wasn't sure what to confess, but my teacher, Sister Mary A., said we should tell the priest everything we had done wrong. I told the priest about disobeying my parents, lying to my brother and not cleaning my room. I really looked forward to my first communion, because then I would be back on "the right track with God again," according to Sister Mary A. I received a white pearl- covered prayer book with a white tassel in second grade. Sister Mary A. said if I ever committed a mortal sin I would need to cut the tassel off. I could never envision myself doing such a wrong, so I decided not to worry about it. But if I died with a mortal sin on my soul, I would go straight to hell.

But by age nine, I believed it was time to cut my tassel off. I went to confession and started as usual:

"Bless me, Father, for I have sinned. My girlfriend and I looked at each other underneath our blouses to see if we were developing breasts yet," I admitted.

"You are on the road to hell, you know. You could easily end up there. In fact, you are probably almost there now," Monsignor said.

He paused, reflecting on how evil I had become. He finally added, "Say five Our Fathers and three Hail Mary's and go and sin no more. Your sins are forgiven."

I don't remember focusing on the "forgiven" aspect as much as the "road to hell" part. I had never felt so hopeless about myself. Looking at my friend's breast didn't feel like a mortal sin but it must have been bad enough to cut off the white tassel. Monsignor didn't mention the tassel. Maybe I'd leave it on, if no one else knew of my sin. God knew. I still couldn't bring myself to cut off the white tassel.

As soon I learned I was going to hell, I felt sick to my stomach. I remember my skirt suddenly felt too tight. I couldn't breathe right. But I had to play my clarinet in a concert at the park a few minutes from then, so I had no time to be sick. I never told my parents. I didn't want them to know how evil their daughter had become. I fought the urge to vomit throughout the concert. How do you tell your parents you're going to hell?

Soon after the confession, the nightmares started. I dreamt about hell and Dante's Inferno for many nights. The nuns had been quick to describe the tortures in hell. I woke up with bloody scratches on my abdomen. Each night became agony as I tried to escape from hell. My mom wondered why I scratched myself so much in the night. I never did tell her.

I became an excellent speller to win laminated holy cards that had "ejaculations" printed on the back side of a saint's picture, short prayers that took up to 365 days of purgatory off your sentence of suffering before you were cleansed enough to enter heaven. I said these short prayers every night till I would fall asleep. Once I won a spelling bee and received a new holy card that said I could take seven years off purgatory simply for reverently saying, "Jesus, Mary, and Joseph."

By the time I was twelve years old, I was learning to be curious about sex. Many admonishments were given on a daily basis at school. Modesty, chastity and purity were the greatest virtues. We needed to be extra careful if we went swimming. Girls and women were the sources of all temptation and evil. If I had any hopes of not going to hell, the nuns worked hard to erase them. I still didn't cut off my white tassel.

My mom didn't discuss sex with me, but once left a brochure under my pillow entitled, "Ann Landers talks to teens about sex." It was better than nothing, but I remember thinking it was not a safe topic to talk about with others.

My mom did resort to talking about sex the day before I was to start high school. She must have felt compelled to.

I sat on the edge of my bed. I looked at my lavender walls and the large flowers on my drapes in multiple shades of purple and lavender. I looked everywhere but at my mom's face.

"Do you know what rape is?" she asked.

"No," I said. She didn't need to know that Suzy Miller had told me about it two days before.

"Well, it's when a man forces you to have sex with him. Don't let it happen to you." It was an order, not a warning.

"OK," I said. My sex education was complete. I was off to high school.

CHAPTER 2

Paul and Our Early Years

Public high school was both a treat and a challenge. I liked having multiple teachers, lockers and bells ringing between classes. I took school seriously. Playing clarinet and twirling baton for our high school band were my favorite activities, but I also found boys interesting. My first crush ended in heartbreak after Jeremy told me he had found someone else he wanted to date. I cried for days.

One day during my sophomore year, I noticed Paul as he walked through the fire doors on the second floor. He had beautiful blue eyes, long eyelashes, wavy dark hair and a cute tush on a six -foot frame. He looked like *Wally Cleaver on Leave it to Beaver*. I felt a battle raging between my hormones and my desire to avoid "impure thoughts," as the nuns called them. Any natural attraction to the opposite sex qualified. The chemistry was good for me, but I didn't know if it would be reciprocated.

A few weeks after I first noticed Paul, I attended a class party at the nearby lake. I joined a group of kids where a dozen girls were encircled around Paul wanting to hold his kerosene hand warmer. The evening was chilly and he had brought the right accessory. I joined the group and started chatting away. After awhile, several girls moved off with different guys and I found myself alone with Paul. He invited me to walk around the lake with him. This walk began a thirty-two- year odyssey that neither of us could have foreseen.

We began seeing each other frequently, sometimes on a group date, sometimes walking home after school. His father had died the previous year. Paul was the chief breadwinner for a family of five. His mother counted on him and his younger brother to run the family farm and work a part -time job at a gas station. No wonder he seemed so mature to me. He had adult responsibilities and was the father figure for his two little sisters and younger brother. I was impressed by his care and commitment to his family, not realizing that Paul was paying a heavy price for having his childhood come to such an abrupt halt.

My parents liked Paul. My father could relate to him, since he, too, had lost a father when he was fourteen, within two weeks of the 1929 stock market crash and the Great Depression. My dad had been the sole breadwinner for a family of four, so he and Paul had a common bond. My mom also liked Paul. Paul was good to his mom and mine. He was respectful, kind and handsome. Everyone liked him.

Our goals were quite different, however. Paul didn't really know what he wanted to do after high school, and I had grown up with the notion that I would go to college. I wasn't sure what I would study, but I knew I was going. Paul's grades weren't the best, largely due to his working so much. He didn't have much time to study after football, choir and work. Over the next few months, I noticed Paul taking a more serious interest in school and his grades. He stopped getting D's and began getting C's and B's. He began to consider college in his future.

By our junior year Paul and I were steadily dating. We exchanged class rings. He gave me my first "movie star" kiss. I called it a "movie star" kiss because it was filled with passion and wasn't a peck on the cheek like I got from my relatives. It was a full-blown, luscious kiss that changed my world as I had previously known it. My parents must have noticed. I started hearing warnings and cautionary tales from my mom.

"Don't get too serious too soon," she said.

"Don't worry, Mom." I assured her.

"Well, last night, I know you were sitting outside on the porch swing until ten o'clock. It doesn't look right. What do you think the neighbors were thinking?"

"Well, they're probably thinking I have a boyfriend I really like."

"No, it's more serious than that. They could be thinking you are flirting with major problems if you are not listening to your parents and getting in at a decent hour."

Mom tried valiantly to deflect her worries and concerns onto the prying eyes of our neighbors.

"You've got a long time to date before you settle on one boy, you know." She gave me a penetrating glance. I'm not sure what she expected me to say, but I knew I was falling seriously in love at fifteen years old and paid little attention to her cautious words. How could mom know anything about love?

I tried to wrap up this winless dialogue.

"All right, Mom. I'll try not to worry you so much." I found being agreeable was the best and easiest stance to take. This posture would prove my undoing in later years.

My dad kept still. He probably didn't know what to say. If he was worried, he tried his best not to show concern. He'd rarely shown me any physical affection. He didn't hug me, pat me on the back or even tease me. He gave me a dollar for every report card I brought home. They were usually very good report cards, and he always paid me and complimented me for the work I did, even if I'd hit a rough spot. It was a big motivator. He was a good and responsible dad, but he was not demonstrative. The male attention I received from Paul filled a huge void in my life. I felt more cared for than I ever had before. It was powerful.

By our junior year in high school, Paul and I had decided to attend community college together, even though I'd been accepted to some highly competitive universities. We also planned to finish school and then marry. While getting an education, Paul and I both worked part-time jobs. I noticed he was often exhausted on our dates, but between constant study and work, it was understandable. He drank alcohol, but so did I by age eighteen. This was the norm in our day, to drink while still under twenty-one. The sixties were not much different from today with regard to alcohol consumption.

We followed through with our plan and married two weeks after our college graduation. We were teachers now. Paul taught at the high school, I at the elementary school. Material belongings weren't high on our priority list. We lived in a small town in a mobile home for the first three years of our marriage, fifteen miles from our roots. We had parents and relatives very close by. We were very happy and spent the next three summers attending graduate school in Colorado. We enjoyed working with other young teachers, who were filled with energy and idealism like ourselves.

Three years after our wedding, Paul's mom died from breast cancer at age fifty-two, after being a widow for many years. We buried her on Mother's Day in 1971. She had decided to ignore her symptoms and not treat her cancer until it was too late. My mom died from stomach carcinoma three months later at the age of forty-eight. We skipped our graduation ceremonies in Colorado to be with my mom in her final days. Her malignant tumor had been too large to treat or remove by the time it had been discovered. We both had lost our mothers in one summer. Paul and I were filled with grief.

We soon moved to a large suburban school district. We were armed with our master's degrees and enjoyed the new opportunities that followed. Paul started teaching in a community college, and I taught third grade and became pregnant with our first child. Ann was born in August, a year after our mothers had died. We wished they could have seen her and been doting grandmas, but we were thrilled for ourselves, as was my father. Ann was healthy, bright and beautiful. I couldn't have wished for more. I decided I would stay home with her and told my school district I would not be returning in the fall.

One Sunday, Paul and I were leaving church walking to the parking lot. He held Ann cradled in his arms and started to skip ahead of me, like kindergarteners do on a playground. I thought it was nice for him to feel so joyful and uninhibited. It was many years later that I put this behavior into a larger framework. His euphoric and slightly inappropriate behavior indicated the surfacing of a bigger problem.

My dad started dating after awhile. It felt strange when he called to tell me about women he'd seen. He didn't give me intimate details, but he did like to tell me about his dates and his reactions to them. He was lost without my mom, even though they'd had a turbulent marriage. He didn't know much about cleaning or cooking or any of the traditional roles my mom filled. By the time our daughter, Ann, was three months old my dad had remarried. We were all blessed he had chosen a lovely woman and friend of my mom's. She was an excellent choice.

When Ann was almost eighteen months old, I started teaching an introductory psychology course at our local community college one night a week. It felt good to continue teaching, even in a minimal way. I enjoyed the intellectual challenge. I loved being a mom to my beautiful daughter, but I needed to use my mind in other ways. I can still see Ann sitting in her high chair after supper crying as I left to teach my first class. I felt guilty for leaving her, nervous about my first college class and excited at the same time. Paul was encouraging. We both knew Ann would be all right once she got used to me leaving one night a week.

When I think back on those early days now, I remember them being filled with optimism. Oh, God, anything was possible. Paul was working hard to individualize instruction for his students. I felt proud of him and our daughter. Our goals were so in tune with each other. We enjoyed parenting, teaching and becoming new homeowners. We mistrusted "the establishment" during college and now we were "them."

By the time Ann was almost a year old we were faced with another extended family crisis. Paul's fifteen -year -old sister Janie was left an orphan when her mom died. During the first year on their own, Paul's younger brother Len managed to care for her in their family home while he attended college during the day and she went to high school. It concerned me, since she was on her own and alone so much at a very vulnerable age. Paul wanted to give his younger brother a year being a surrogate parent, but it was obvious the plan wasn't working well.

Paul broached the subject first. "Carol, I think we should offer Janie a home. She's too much responsibility for my brother."

"Would she want to come live with us, go to a new high school her sophomore year, and leave her friends? Is she willing to come?" I asked all at once.

Paul thought for a moment and said, "I'm not sure she wants to come, but I think leaving her in the current situation with Len is inviting real trouble. She's noticing boys, taking off in cars with guys Len doesn't know. He thinks she's experimenting with pot."

"I'm afraid she'll be very upset to leave the only home she's ever known. She's probably not too happy with me for taking away the only father figure she's ever known," I said. I pictured a very rebellious, grief-filled, angry teen coming our way.

"This won't be easy," Paul said, "but we need to offer our home and at least try. I wouldn't feel right leaving her without adequate supervision and letting her get in more and more trouble. Her grades are falling already. What do you say?"

"All right, Paul. I know I can never replace her mom, but I could be a supportive adult and do my best to give her a home, set limits and let her know we really care about her," I said. "She's always been so close to you and has such mixed feelings about me. But I've always liked Janie and would do my best for her."

"Good," Paul said. "I'll call my brother tonight and we'll take this in steps. I'd like to make sure she's here for awhile in the summer, so she can register in time for the next school year."

CHAPTER 3

Discontent

It was a hot August night. I had just passed the parmesan cheese to Paul as we ate supper in our dining room when Janie burst in through our back door. Len had dropped her off with two shabby suitcases and a few paper bags. It was all she owned. She was crying. Ann stared at her from her high chair, spaghetti sauce smeared across her face from ear to ear.

"You've got to help me find him!" she screamed.

"Find who?" I asked, puzzled. I didn't know we were expecting anyone else.

"Sammy, my cat. He jumped out of the car out front!" she wailed.

"Let's go out in the yard and look around," Paul said. "He couldn't have gone far." He went with Janie in a search of Sammy.

Many tears and moments of anguish later, the cat was found. I showed Janie her new bedroom, which I had tried to make inviting to a teenager. Len drove home and Janie unpacked.

Ann was a calming and distracting influence. She and Ann clicked immediately which helped to redirect the evening's emotional tone. Thank God for little children: Ann was magical in her ability to help Janie settle into her new room. Her funny expressions and mispronounced words had Janie laughing in minutes.

Janie's good humor was short- lived. Once school started, we began to hear the complaints about missing old friends, "stuck-up" kids in our town and the teachers who knew nothing. Paul and I tried to be reassuring and encouraged her to be patient. We were very aware of how difficult this could be for a fifteen-year-old who had no parents to comfort her. But we felt we were better surrogates than foster care parents would be, so we tried to listen and be the best inexperienced parents we could be at the age of twenty-seven. But sometimes hopes and expectations have little connection to outcomes.

Janie turned to alcohol and other drugs to ease her pain of having become an orphan at fourteen. Many years later, I learned Paul and his younger brother had often told Janie her parents were crazy for having her. They were struggling with three children—why would they bring another child into the world? And then they both died so young. Unbeknownst to me, Janie was shouldering this additional burden and not confiding in anyone. Incredible, emotional pain resulting from these statements added to her grief.

What I wasn't prepared for was Janie leaving "speed" pills on the clothes dryer, within Ann's reach if she stood on a stool. We found our family car parked in front of a bar one evening, not at the library where Janie had told us she was going. Her dean called more than once to tell us she had been suspended for smoking in the girls' restroom. Conflicts were escalating daily. We decided to try family therapy.

Our attempt at family therapy was not successful. Our therapist was relatively inexperienced and our opening session foretold the future.

The therapist began with me.

"Please tell me your first name," he said.

"Carol," I replied.

"How do you spell that?"

"C-a-r-o-l."

"Is there an *e* at the end of it?"

"No," I said. "Plain C-a-r-o-l."

"So, how long have you thought of yourself as plain?" he asked.

"I don't think I'm plain. I'm trying to clarify my first name's spelling. We are really here to try and help Janie, who is struggling to cope with losing both of her parents," I said.

"I think we need to go back and talk more about why you see yourself as plain, Carol."

At this juncture, I lost total interest in family therapy and reminded myself never to do this to my clients when I began working as a therapist. We didn't return after he spent a miserable hour questioning us. Neither Paul nor I were impressed, but now we felt more hopeless. And now I was wondering about being "plain."

I continued ruminating about our family session and started preparing supper.

I removed my rings and washed my hands in the kitchen sink. Then I plunged my fingers into the bowl of ground beef with chopped onions and green peppers to start my favorite meat loaf.

"Do you know how bad red meat is for your heart?" Janie asked me, as I continued blending the ingredients.

"Do you know how harmful cigarettes are for your lungs?" I countered, deciding to wait on the pot and speed lecture.

Although I had completed my training to become a counselor, I was not feeling like one in this capacity. I didn't have a clue about how to be a substitute parent.

Janie grew alfalfa sprouts in my kitchen cupboards. She believed in herbal tea power. She was fascinated with organic foods and healthy menus, but couldn't understand why we didn't approve of illicit drugs. Her grades were less than stellar, but she was making friends. We weren't always sure who her friends were, however, since she met them at school functions and she rarely brought anyone home for us to meet.

One morning, I mentioned to Paul my growing discomfort with Janie's behavior.

"I feel like a stranger in my own kitchen, Paul. Janie tells me what to cook and what foods she considers unhealthy, but she has no problem smoking cigarettes and pot. I know we're still grieving our moms' deaths, but she's a mess. She doesn't give a damn about school," I said.

"Well, what do you want me to do about it? You're the shrink. You tell me. I'm tired of you both complaining. Wait till she's eighteen. I'll be happy to tell her to leave on her eighteenth birthday," he said.

"Paul, she's your sister. We can't ignore her. She loves the baby, but I can't allow Ann to ride in the car with her, because I can't trust what she'll do. But Janie gets angry when I tell her she can't drive the car. I need support from you when I have to tell her 'no.'"

Silence. Paul tended to become silent when I needed connection and sharing the most. I didn't expect us to have identical feelings, but he used silence as punishment when he didn't agree with me, which was very powerful. He knew it. I refused to let it incapacitate me. I would do what I could for Janie, but I would not sacrifice our own daughter or jeopardize her health and safety. I would also postpone my desire for another child until Janie was launched. I couldn't see adding a child to our family right now.

In 1974 the stock market dropped like a stone and Paul felt some panic. He walked through the kitchen door one Friday afternoon after leaving work. He announced "I'm driving to New York City tonight and will be back before I have to be at work on Monday morning. I need to take possession of $10,000 worth of quarters. I've decided against silver or gold bouillon."

"Paul, are you sure you need to do this? It sounds pretty drastic. I know you're worried about the market, but New York? Over the weekend? The roundtrip from here would be almost fifteen hundred miles! When will you sleep? What kind of neighborhood would you be in? I'm frightened for you. Are you that scared about the economy?"

"I'll be fine. I'll pull off the side of the road if I get drowsy. Carol, I need to do this now, before the whole economy is ruined. Trust me. I know what I'm doing. I'll be fine. This is the best way to protect our assets."

He walked into the great room and sat by the phone and dialed. I overheard him talking to a broker about puts and calls, options, futures and commodities. I knew he was serious about this.

He left despite my protests and pleas. I was so worried about him, but he was convinced he needed to do this.

He arrived home late Sunday night, quite dishevelled, wearing the same clothes he had worn at the start of the trip. The back of our pick-up truck was loaded with many white plastic buckets filled with quarters. He hauled them down to the basement one at a time. They were so heavy I couldn't help him. It seemed strange to have possession of $10,000 worth of quarters. I was so relieved to have him home, safe and sound. I fell asleep immediately. Paul claimed he wasn't very tired and he decided to stay up longer. What energy!

The day finally arrived when Janie graduated from high school and turned eighteen. We felt a mixture of sadness and relief. She had decided to be a massage therapist and go to school in Oregon. She left and succeeded in her goal. She was able to return to our town and practice her profession for many years. Any doubts about her career goals were replaced with pride.

The best news was I was pregnant. We were having a baby in November of 1976. A bicentennial baby. We were both thirty years old and couldn't be happier. Max was born and he was healthy and contented. Paul was very glad to have a son and I was elated. Ann was four by now and quite the little helper. We felt very blessed to have two healthy children. We always wished our parents could have all survived to see them. They would have loved being grandparents.

Paul was teaching and also selling real estate during the summer months. As we laid in bed one hot, summer night in 1977, we looked outside into the darkness through the open screened window, pillows propped under our chins. It was so still out, except for the crickets.

Paul broke the stillness. "I want to retire by the time I'm thirty-five," he said.

I blinked in disbelief as he continued.

"I don't want to be teaching and selling real estate until I'm old."

"What would you do instead?" I asked.

"I don't really know. I'd like to do what I really want to do, and that doesn't involve what I'm doing now."

"Hmm …. Well, I don't expect us to become rich. I want to be able to provide for ourselves and the kids, but I don't need you to make a big fortune. I can help with some additional income when the kids get into school. I plan on helping you more with money," I continued.

"Well, good, but I plan to retire in five years," Paul said.

I laughed. I thought this was a very unrealistic goal, unless we won the lottery.

"Let me know, Paul, when you have the early retirement thing figured out. Until then, I'll keep doing what I need to do."

CHAPTER 4

Seeds of Doubt

I stopped teaching psychology at our community college when Max was born, but by the time he was two, I was getting itchy to work somewhere beyond home. I didn't want to work more than two hours a week, however. It sounds laughable now, but I found the perfect job. The hours were right: two hours a week. The pay was not good: zero dollars. I would be a volunteer at a community mental health agency, but thought it could turn into a real job someday. I would be an individual, marriage and family therapist. It was a young and emerging profession, but I was intrigued. I wanted the opportunity to learn all I could.

I loved my new volunteer position and enjoyed the people I worked with. Licensure was not yet available in our field for our state, so the agency accepted my master's in psychology as sufficient. I enjoyed the challenge of working with individuals, couples and families who came through our doors. What an opportunity. By the time Max was four, it turned into a real job, and I got a decent hourly wage, four to six hours a week.

Paul completed an amazing real estate transaction and sold farm land to ten doctors from India wanting to build a Hindu temple. His commission was impressive, enough to encourage us to look for a larger home for our growing family. We found one in the adjacent community before it was publicly listed. The house on Treetop Lane was in a great neighborhood within an excellent school district. We were eager to make an offer and get a closing date before the next school year began. I felt as though I were living in my "dream movie." We were able to close quickly and left on the same day for my brother's wedding in Michigan. We were all in the ceremony and our spirits were high. I remember the summer of 1980 as the best in our family's history.

I've spent long hours trying to figure out when our marriage started taking a turn for the worse. I would think I'd have greater clarity about the demise of my own marriage, since I'd been trained and eventually licensed to help others with their relationship difficulties. One might expect me to have a loving, vital and committed marriage. I believed this as well. I enjoyed watching couples I worked with grow stronger in their relationships. I often reminded them they were the captains of their ship, and I would help serve as their navigator. This was a good metaphor. I also used one about giving them more "tools for their toolbox," which was quite appealing to men. I took pleasure in helping others rescue themselves from divorce.

I felt so lucky on Valentine's Day, 1982. I found Paul's note to me.

My Dearest Valentine,

I love you more now as ever before. The very best of days would be nothing without you.

You give me so much and ask so little in return. You warm my nights and days and make me tingle with anticipation of your voice as I start home each day. You make me proud, so very proud, that you have asked me to be your Valentine. I accept!

XXX
OOO
Paul

By the fall of 1983, Max, who was almost seven, played soccer for a community park district team. I noticed Paul sleeping through most of Max's soccer games. I would make him strong coffee and pour it into a thermos. I felt irritated at Paul for sleeping and I tried to cheer and make enough noise for the two of us, so Max wouldn't notice. When Max would catch Paul asleep, I'd remind him about Dad's long hours and difficult job. I felt annoyed at Paul and finally quit making excuses for him.

This planted tiny "doubt" seeds in my mind. I tried not to let the seeds grow. It was too frightening to think about.

One night after I'd gone to bed, I awoke when Paul arrived home late from a meeting. I was half asleep, but heard him in our closet changing clothes. It sounded as though he bumped into a wall on his way to bed, but I was so tired I didn't stir. I heard water streaming. I looked up to see Paul urinating into his sock drawer. I was shocked, but rolled back to sleep, knowing this conversation would wait until morning.

When Paul woke up, I said, "Paul, you peed in your sock drawer last night, and I don't plan to clean it up."

"What the hell? I did not. I would never do that," he said.

"You wouldn't do it sober. But I think you might have had too much to drink after your meeting last night, and pissed in your sock drawer."

"I can't believe this shit," he said. He walked to the dresser and opened his sock drawer. He closed it in disgust. "All right. Maybe I made a mistake. Must have thought I was in the other room. I'll clean it up."

He cleaned in silence for a half hour.

When he finished I asked him if he would consider going to see a marriage and family therapist with me.

"Hell no! You know everyone of them in town. I know they'd be biased against me. It wouldn't be fair."

"I don't know all the therapists in town, but you are right. I know a lot of them. We could go out of town. You choose who we see. At least think about it. I want our marriage to thrive and we are struggling."

"One little mistake last night doesn't mean we need therapy." He walked away and refused to discuss it again.

Overall, the kids were doing well with school and friends. I'd developed a great method of focusing on pleasant things instead of the difficult. It was as though I wanted to be in a feature film called "The Sound of Music" and not this life with harsher realities.

Ann was hitting adolescence, and the physical changes were quickly showing, so fifth grade started out with some teasing from boys. She claimed she wanted to quit school and she was very serious. Fortunately, she was blessed with a great principal, who stopped the teasing by confronting the instigators. Ann's school year improved. I wish I could say the same for our marriage.

CHAPTER 5

Restless

Sometime in the 1983 school year, Paul complained of getting restless at his college teaching post. A new president had been hired, and there was much unrest with union members. He spent many nights on the phone talking about strategies with his teacher-union colleagues. A strike ensued and it was a tense time. I had enjoyed the camaraderie with faculty and administrative wives, but those days were short-lived. Attending teas and luncheons at the home of the former president became dim memories.

I noticed Paul pouring himself a drink as soon as he came home from work and again later while he talked on the phone with his friends in the evening. I hadn't noticed him drinking this much before.

A few weeks later, Paul shocked me one evening in the kitchen while I prepared one of the kids' favorite dishes for supper.

"I've been thinking about quitting teaching," he said.

"Really? I'm surprised. You've always loved teaching, except for the politics. Or so I thought."

"Don't say *really*. You say the word too much. I hate the word. I don't like teaching at all anymore," he continued.

"What would you like to do instead?" I hoped there was an *instead*.

"I have an opportunity to start my own business, a machine tool shop with a guy I already know and like. He and I have done some real estate deals together. He's got an office nearby. He wants to get started pretty soon and I told him I might be interested in being his partner. I think this sounds very promising."

"Wow. It would be a big change for you, Paul, after fourteen years of teaching, but it's important to like what you do. I don't want you being unhappy every day. So, if this is what you want to do, I'll support you. What's the guy's name? Do I know him?" I asked.

"No, I don't think you've ever met him or even heard me talk about Jim. This idea is pretty fresh, so it's still new, even to me."

"Well, give it some thought, Paul. If this is really what you want to do, go ahead. Otherwise, you'll always wonder," I said.

"Yeah, we're going to meet for a drink next week. I'll know more then and try to nail down some details. He's a good guy. Good reputation in the community. I think I could learn a lot from him."

"Sounds good. You sound happier than you have in a long time. I hope it all works out."

Paul was on tenure at the college, but decided to turn in his resignation before the next school term. He was feeling confident about his new business venture with Jim. It would be small at first, but their hope was to grow the business.

It felt strange at first to have Paul head out in a different direction for work in the morning. He seemed happier and optimistic, like a huge burden had been lifted. I had underestimated what a toll the teaching job had been taking on him. At the age of thirty-seven, it was a good time to make a career move. He wasn't yet forty, so why not?

I had started working more hours for our community mental health agency. I liked the work and my colleagues. I began acquiring the supervision hours needed to become a clinical member of the American Association for Marriage and Family Therapy. I took courses needed for this honor, since back in the 60s, there were no MFT tracks at universities and colleges. I had to accumulate the necessary course work in a piecemeal fashion, but it was worth my time and effort. I was passionate about helping troubled marriages and families. I enjoyed the work and felt it a privilege to work with others and give them the hope and courage to change.

CHAPTER 6

And All Through the House There Was Fear

Christmas was quickly approaching, my favorite holiday. Max had turned seven in November and Ann was already eleven. They were very bright and healthy and had the shiniest black hair, just like their Swedish grandmother. I had enrolled Ann in an etiquette class and she loved it. She learned how to model on a runway and really enjoyed it. She modeled in fashion shows for Sears, J.C. Penny and Marshall Field's.

Paul's new business venture had been under way for a couple months when he suggested we invite his business partner, wife and family over for a pre-holiday dinner. Despite not having our Christmas tree up yet, our home looked very festive. I selected two different menus, one appealing to the adults and one for the four children. The dishes were pearly milk glass and a sharp contrast to the crimson tablecloth on the Queen Anne table. I could smell the aromatic pine boughs I had threaded through our brass Williamsburg chandelier in the dining room. I polished my Kirk Stieff Repousse sterling silver and hand washed the crystal until it sparkled. The room looked as pretty as any I had seen on a magazine cover. At the time, appearances were more important to me then than they are now. I learned that having fun and a good time always trumps appearances, but I was different back then.

The dinner itself was a success as far as the food went. I noticed Paul was drinking far more wine than usual; his eyes were red and glassy. He started talking very deliberately and slurring his words. I wanted the dinner to finish quickly at this point, before Paul did or said something he'd later regret in front of his new business partner.

Paul pointed at Max sitting two chairs away from him. "Like I was sayin', Max is improving at soccer. Helluvalot better'n when he started," Paul said with a hiccup.

I wondered if our guests noticed the ponderous and slow words as much as I had. I also wondered how Paul knew Max was improving, since he'd slept through so many games.

I saw Jim wink at his wife when he thought no one was looking; he seemed delighted with Paul's inebriation.

I flicked my wrist mid-air to get everyone's attention. "May I interest anyone in dessert and coffee?" I asked, hoping to move this ill-fated affair along. "I have cherry cheesecake with whipped cream or peppermint ice cream," I added. "Regular or decaf' coffee?"

After dessert and coffee, Paul's partner yawned and suggested the kids begin picking up. He needed to get up early the next morning. I felt grateful for his suggestion and tried not to breathe an audible sigh of relief. Jim and his wife gathered their children and toys together before saying good-bye.

Their young son Tim said, "Where is my toy airplane? I can't find it!" We all began searching the house, but with no luck.

I made a suggestion. "When I clean tomorrow I'll probably find it, and I'll send it back with Paul when he goes to work." Good-byes were exchanged and we sent Ann and Max to their rooms to get ready for bed.

Once the door closed behind our guests, I watched Paul as he bolted up the stairs and head for Max's room. I could hear him yelling. Paul had always been a good father, but, I felt frightened. He'd had way too much to drink.

"Why did you steal the airplane, Max?" he asked. "I'm not raising a thief. Now find it and give it to me immediately."

"But Dad, I didn't take it. I don't know where it is. Please believe me, Dad!" Max pleaded.

I could hear Paul growl more accusations. I ran up the stairs and saw him shaking Max. Max started crying as I approached.

"Paul, don't shake him. I'm sure the airplane will turn up tomorrow, and I'm also sure Max would never steal it. Stop shaking him."

Paul stopped shaking him. I tried to comfort Max and helped him get into bed. I was sure he wouldn't have an easy time getting to sleep, but I needed to deal with Paul and diffuse his anger. Paul followed me downstairs, into the kitchen, almost running. I turned around and looked straight at him. His eyes were red and vacant.

He launched at me. "You've never loved me," he began, his words more slurred than before. He pushed me and stumbled. I was frightened. Never had I seen him like this.

"That's ridiculous!" I screamed. "I have loved you faithfully since we were fifteen years old. We've had so many good years together! I can't believe you're saying this."

My protestations fell on deaf ears. I was having a conversation with the alcohol. Paul grabbed the coffee pot and smashed it on the floor. He ran toward the banister in the foyer and pushed and pulled it back and forth, trying to rip it out. He had just repaired it the previous weekend. I heard the beautiful hardwood snap.

I ran toward the phone on the kitchen wall to call 911. He grabbed the phone from my hand and tore it off the wall. Paul knelt down and started smashing his head into the pegged oak floor. His forehead dripped with blood. I looked at him in total disbelief, more afraid than I'd ever been in my life. The scene was surreal. Any moment I would wake up and Paul would be back to his good-natured self. I didn't know what to do. I wasn't prepared for this. I didn't have an emergency bag packed like the one I recommended for my clients. This had never occurred in my home. Did I think I was I exempt, this would never happen to me? I felt the fear and dread associated with domestic violence. Things happened so fast. I barely had time to think.

I offered Paul a clean dishcloth to mop the blood from his head. He pushed it away. He refused any help. Would he try to hurt me now? Would he try to hurt Max? What about Ann? I hoped she was asleep. I hoped Max was asleep. I don't think they could have been. Paul and I never fought like this, and never in front of the children. We didn't believe in involving the kids in our disputes, and we rarely had serious disagreements.

How should I get help? I could run next door and ask our neighbors to call the police. If I went for the door, I didn't think Paul would let me leave. I'm sure he wouldn't want the neighbors to know and he'd try to stop me. And if I did make it out, who would be there to protect the kids? I felt trapped with no phone. If I could get to another phone in the house …. Maybe the others weren't dead. While Paul mopped his forehead, I quietly went to the living room and picked up the phone. It was also dead.

I walked back into the kitchen, trying to look unafraid even though my heart was racing. Paul was crying. He walked in silence to the family room sofa and lied down. Within seconds he was asleep. I walked upstairs to check on the kids. They were either both asleep or pretending to be. I thought about waking them and taking them to a shelter. We would probably have to stay over the holiday. It would be a bad memory that would taint all future Christmas holidays. But then I thought, *this memory had already scarred them.*

I decided I would talk with Paul in the morning once he'd sobered up. I didn't feel we were in harm's way once he was sleeping. I resolved I wouldn't live like this, since it violated all of my religious and moral training. But I wouldn't give up on my marriage this easily, not after sixteen good years. Paul needed help. I would give him an ultimatum regarding his drinking and behavior, because I would not repeat this night. The children and I would not live in a house where we were threatened or felt unsafe.

The next morning Paul slept until 9:30, late for a guy who liked waking before sunrise. I was pleased when he mentioned his headache. I thought a good hangover might be a prelude to acknowledging he had a problem. He was not overly contrite due to a partial memory blackout. I filled in the missing details. He looked perplexed when he viewed the broken phone, banister and coffeepot.

"What the hell happened down here?" he asked.

"You had a rough night, Paul. I guess you don't remember, but you got pretty ugly with Max and me. You scared us both. I'm sure Ann was frightened as well. I've never seen you drink so much and then behave so badly afterwards. You did some damage and refused to let me call for help. That's why the phone is pulled out of the wall. I will never endure a night like that again. I won't wait around for you to disconnect the phone. I will take the kids and leave you."

He looked stunned and was in total disbelief over what he'd done. He tapped his forehead where the blood had dried and caked on. He walked to the bathroom and looked in the mirror.

"What the …? How did it happen? Did you hit me?"

"No, but the thought of it had some appeal last night. You smashed your head into the wood floor and told me I didn't love you. I'm not sure where your notions sprang from, but you were very drunk."

"I guess I should put a Band-Aid on before the kids come down. I don't think I need stitches, but damn, it's sore," he said.

I pointed my index finger at him. "I still love you, but I have conditions if I'm to stay with you. At the very least, you need to repair the damage you inflicted on Max last night. He needs a heartfelt apology for starters. You need help for your drinking. If you ever do this again, I'll have no choice but to leave you, file for divorce and take the kids. It's not what I want, but I'll do it if all else fails," I said.

"I'm not sure what happened," Paul replied, shaking his head. "I guess I wanted to impress my partner and his family. I didn't want a stupid toy airplane destroying my new partnership. I can stop drinking on my own. I don't need any help with it. I don't need alcohol. I'll stop. I don't want you to leave me. I won't do it again. I'll clean up the mess downstairs." His shoulders slumped and his head hung low as he continued, "Now leave me alone. I don't want to talk now."

Paul disappeared into the basement to get some tools and start the repairs. He hadn't given me the apology I'd hoped for, but he was remorseful and taking some responsibility for what he did. He promised to quit drinking, but I wasn't convinced he could spontaneously stop. And although he was ashamed of his behavior, I had hoped for reassurances that he loved the kids and me. I was naïve in hoping his love for us would be enough to motivate him to accept help, but at the time, I thought it was the best I could expect. I accepted his words with reservations, relief and hope. I was concerned about alcoholism at the time, not whether Paul might be self-medicating a mental health problem.

A few days later, I came home from work and found Max and Ann both very upset, trying to talk at once.

"Why did Daddy throw the Christmas tree down the hill, Mom?" Ann asked.

I couldn't answer her. I couldn't believe it. I looked out the living room window and down our steep hill and saw the tree resting at the end of the driveway. It was almost hidden from view, partially covered in snow from sliding into a snowdrift. I hadn't seen it as I'd come up the drive. I looked for Paul and could hear sawing in the garage.

I walked slowly to the garage door trying to formulate the words I would say. "Paul, why is our Christmas tree resting at the bottom of our driveway?" I asked.

"It was crooked. It didn't sit well in the stand," he said matter-of-factly.

"Well, the kids are heartbroken and scared. Why did you need to throw it down the driveway? The tree means a lot to them. We were all looking forward to decorating it this weekend." He kept on sawing wood.

He ignored me and my comment. I went inside the house. I hated the silent power game he played.

"OK, kids. Get your coats on. Let's go down the driveway and we'll drag the tree up the hill. I think I'll need your help since it's pretty big."

"Why did Daddy throw out our tree, Mom?" Max asked.

"Honey, I don't really know. Your daddy's been stressed lately about his new job. I don't think he knows how he hurts you when he does things like that. But don't worry. I'll put the tree back in the stand and I'll make it pretty again."

And I did. After I fixed our tree, I went upstairs to our bedroom to look at the lighted luminerias outlining the sidewalks and driveways in our subdivision. Since our home was on the highest hill in town, the view out our bedroom window was spectacular in the evening. I looked down upon the flickering lights in the snow and it took my breath away. It was such a beautiful sight; cold, but peaceful and still. I wished my life could feel as calm. My insides were churning with anger and fear.

I wanted to put my marriage back into place and make it solid again. I wanted to make it pretty again, like the tree. I vowed to stay with Paul and give him time to set things right. I didn't feel I could leave or divorce him because of one or two nightmarish events. Love within marriage was not a feeling; it was a commitment. Our vows included "in sickness and in health," and this was the "in sickness" part. But it takes two to honor those vows, and I felt like I was trying to hold on alone. But I also had the feeling the kids and I were riding a runaway train and I needed to jump off and take them with me, but was fearful I'd land on the tracks. We were going at full speed and a wreck was about to occur. But I chose to stay with Paul for now. I was the queen of denial. I refused to see Paul's strange behavior as signs of manic-depression.

ACT

2

CHAPTER 7

A Major Interruption

Back when Ann was a toddler, she and I would sometimes meet Paul for a little picnic lunch on campus during his break. It was always fun to see each other midday, and she loved to see Daddy and surprise him. After Max was born, it rarely happened; once the kids were in school it never happened. So, one morning after work I thought I'd surprise Paul at his new job site during his lunch break. It would have to be a fast food break, but I thought it would be fun.

He was busy working on a milling machine. His partner Jim was sitting in the back office. Paul looked up as I approached him. He turned off the machine and removed his safety goggles. "Hi, Paul," I said, not needing to shout since the machine had stopped.

"Hi, Carol," he said as if he were expecting me.

"I thought I'd surprise you on my way home from work. I got off early today and thought it might be fun to have a quick lunch together."

"You know, there was a time when I would have done anything to see you, anytime, day or night. But now you're an interruption to my important work."

I almost stopped breathing. A knife could not have cut my heart more. I could see bursting in on Paul was not a good idea, but there might have been a more civil way to tell me. Who was this man? I didn't realize then how ill Paul was becoming. I still blamed myself for being thoughtless and insensitive to his stressful new job. Some women would have raced over to see a divorce attorney after those words.

I said, "I can see this wasn't a good idea. I'll leave."

"No, we might as well go have lunch as long as you're here. I'll go tell Jim I'll be back in half an hour," he said.

We walked to the Dairy Queen and shared a tense lunch. It had no resemblance to our lunch dates on the green grass at his college campus. This was the new reality, and I needed to accept it.

CHAPTER 8

Goofing Around with Manic Antics: Eighteen Months Later

Paul and I decided to drive into the city and visit a museum/planetarium complex with Max, now eight. I don't remember where Ann was, but she wasn't along. I do remember walking in a large grassy meadow after touring the museum. It was a warm and sunny day and we were having a good time. Paul was running down the hill chasing after Max., playfully kicking him as he ran away from Paul. Then Paul started spitting at Max after taking a long drink of water. It seemed strange and out of character for Paul to treat Max this way. Max didn't appear upset by his dad's behavior, but I wasn't comfortable with it.

"Paul, take it easy." I said. "I don't think Max likes that."

"We're having fun, goofing around. Relax. I don't need your advice on how to be a father."

I watched as they both ran down the hill together and headed for the men's restroom on my right below. I walked around on the grass encircling the restroom for several minutes waiting for them to exit. I wasn't wearing a watch, but I estimated about ten minutes had gone by. Had they crossed the street to look for me? I had lost them.

I enjoyed the warm sun on my face while watching sailboats out on the lake in the distance. After several minutes, I began to wonder where the guys went. Maybe Paul was angry about my comments and walked across the street with Max to cool off. I walked across the street thinking they might have gone to see the lake. I couldn't find them and they weren't near the restrooms behind me either. They'd vanished. I wandered around for about an hour. I had left my purse in the car parked a mile away. I had no money or identification. I started feeling anxious. Had Paul done this on purpose to punish me for sounding critical? I didn't know what to think. I knew I didn't want to be stranded in the city without resources. As more time passed, the more scared I felt.

Our car appeared about the time I had almost given up hope. Paul was driving toward me in the opposite lane where I was walking. I waved my arms. "Where did you go, Paul?" I asked, on the verge of tears.

"We've been looking for you."

"I've been right here for over an hour, walking up and down the same street, looking toward the men's room. I have no money or ID. I thought you'd left me."

"Well, you're foolish. I wouldn't leave you here. You knew I'd come back and find you," he said.

"I wasn't sure. I thought maybe you left me here on purpose because of what I'd said earlier."

"Well, I didn't lose you. You lost us," Paul concluded.

CHAPTER 9

Hilda: Eight Months Later

Paul was still working with Jim in their new enterprise, but growing a bit concerned with the role Jim's wife played in the business. She was serving as the business manager/bookkeeper and handled all of the finances. Some money was not accounted for and Paul felt their profits were stagnant and that maybe she was using the business as her personal bank. I had misgivings from the start, but Paul needed to decide for himself and discuss his concerns with Jim. I busied myself with the kids and my own career and school issues.

My job still allowed me to be home with the kids after school and evenings, but I noticed there was less time to do housework. Ann was twelve and Max was eight. I needed time during the day to study for the post-graduate college courses that would help me become a clinical member of the American Association for

Marriage and Family Therapy. Paul was not available as much due to the extra hours spent at his new entrepreneurial endeavor. I decided a housekeeper every two weeks could be a help without being a great financial burden. Paul agreed. I checked with friends for recommendations and hired Hilda.

Hilda and her year -long employment with us has remained a mystery to me even to this day. I was quick to rush to judgment after finding broken items after she had cleaned. She explained to me at her first interview she would leave bottles and tools on my kitchen table if they needed to be replaced for the next cleaning appointment. She explained her right hand had suffered severe burns and so she couldn't write her "needs" list for me. She would simply leave the used boxes or bottles for me to see and replenish for the next visit. I agreed to provide her with the necessary cleaning equipment. She would tell me her preferred brands.

Hilda loved lemon-oil more than any other product on the market. From her perspective, there was nothing that couldn't be improved in our home with a heavy coating of lemon-oil. We could always tell when we got home if it had been a "Hilda day." Most anyone enjoys the smell of fresh lemons, but the smell of lemon-oil was now overpowering. Every cupboard, table, dresser and shelf had a lemon-oil sheen on it. Even our antique wooden chairs could be considered dangerous if you sat on them the wrong way. Paul mentioned that perhaps Hilda needed to go. I begged for another chance to work with her. I told him I'd explain to her we were happy with her work for the most part, but would appreciate it if she could use less lemon- oil. He agreed to give her another try.

I wrote Hilda a note explaining our concerns, since I would be at class when she came over. I wasn't there to see how my note, which I thought I had carefully and kindly worded, affected her.

Later, as I started to turn off the bedroom light before going to bed, I noticed the lampshade was broken on our antique lamp. The shade was positioned so the actual break in the glass faced the wall, away from me. I had almost missed seeing it. I was surprised and saddened. It would be hard to replace the glass shade. Paul was angry. He accused Hilda of deliberately disguising a broken lamp shade. He said her impaired hand or clumsiness wasn't the issue, but her deception. She should have owned up to the damage and we could have forgiven her, but now he didn't trust her. I told Paul we had no proof Hilda had broken the lampshade. I decided to ask the kids if they knew anything about it.

I showed them the broken shade. Both of them gasped in surprise.

"Do either of you know what happened here? Did one of you break the shade?" I asked.

"No," they answered in unison. They were either innocent or they had cemented a rare bond of sibling loyalty. However, they were generally truthful. That night I called Hilda on the phone to continue my investigation, but Hilda claimed she knew nothing about the broken shade. She reassured me that she would have told me had she broken anything of ours. That had always been her policy.

Hilda returned two weeks later and when she left with her customary empty bottle collection on the kitchen table, I found myself checking to see if one of those bottles might have contained alcohol. I laughed to myself; she wouldn't be so foolish, even if she did have a drinking problem. I inspected the house and noted the diminished smell of lemons. I inhaled sharply when I entered Ann's room. Lying on Ann's pale pink carpet was a multi-colored nest of wires from a gaping hole in her wall. The outlet near the baseboard had been ripped out of the wall. I wasn't sure how much force it would take from a vacuum cleaner to rip out the outlet and pull wires out of the wall. I was very puzzled and Ann was sad to see the mess in her pretty bedroom. I reassured her I would talk to Hilda and get to the bottom of this latest mystery.

As I might have predicted, Hilda had no knowledge of the gutted outlet. Paul worked at repairing the mess in Ann's bedroom, but was more than a little irritated about the quality of the service we were getting. He had already convicted Hilda, despite her pleas of innocence. Paul was convinced Hilda had little control of her one bad hand and to make matters worse, she was very dishonest.

I decided to call my friend who had recommended Hilda, and she had nothing but good things to say about her. She had never suffered any major damages from Hilda's work, and when Hilda had caused a small crack in the dog's bowl, she had replaced it the next week with an even better one. This didn't sound like a woman bent on deception.

Paul told me his patience had been exhausted. He told me he would give her one more opportunity to clean in two weeks, but then I was to terminate her if there was anything even slightly wrong. He was tired of a stranger entering our home and wreaking havoc every time she cleaned for us. If Hilda were at fault, I shared his sentiments. I was growing weary playing detective.

Two weeks later, the problem came to a quick and surprising conclusion. I came home from work in the mid-afternoon before the kids had arrived home from school. A foot of snow covered the ground and the air was frigid from a sharp, north wind. I walked on the sidewalk as I dug the house key out of my purse, focused on not slipping in the snow. As I started to put the key in the lock, I jumped back in disbelief. The door frame was mangled and the front door was sagging and it listed to one side. Snow and cold air were blowing through the house. I entered and tried leaning the door back into a position where it might stay balanced without falling over. I propped it up with a chair on the inside so it wouldn't blow down. I had no idea how to repair a heavy metal front door. I hoped Paul would come home soon.

And then I thought about Hilda. Could she have done this? *How* could she have done this? Hilda was not young, nor was she very strong. This would have taken a strong person to do this much damage to our front door.

Paul came inside after his day at work.

"What the hell happened to the front door?" he asked.

"I'm not sure, but this was Hilda's day to clean, so it doesn't look good for her."

"You need to call her and fire her immediately. This is ridiculous. And we're paying her to come here? I won't put up with this nonsense!" he yelled.

"I'll call her and let her know we won't need her services any longer."

I wondered if she would admit a problem with the front door. I walked to the kitchen and called her on the phone.

"Hilda, did you have a problem with the front door today? It was broken when I arrived home from work. Snow and cold air were rushing in the house and we really can't have that happen," I explained, overstating the obvious.

"Carol, the door was a bit frozen when I came to unlock the house, so I had to give it a little extra push, but I didn't really hurt your door," she said.

"Well, Hilda, it had to be more than a little push to take the door off its hinges. It would take a lot of strength to break a front door made of steel. I must terminate our service with you. I will send you a final check for your work today, but you needn't return in two weeks. I think we should part company. I'm sorry it had to end like this, but we simply can't continue." The front door mystery was baffling to me.

CHAPTER 10

The Cops Will Never Catch Me (One Year Later)

Paul's new machine tool company imploded in less than two years. He finally confronted Jim about the role his wife was playing in their new business. Their financial goals for the first eighteen months fell below their expectations. Jim tried to justify the income and expenditures in the books, but Paul wasn't reassured. He let Jim know he was unhappy and not fully trusting of his wife's ability to manage things. Paul even suggested they hire an outside person, so there would be more control and transparency over the monetary end of their endeavor. Jim was offended and trust eroded quickly between them.

"I think Jim's wife is siphoning funds away from our business. Jim made her our bookkeeper because she needed a part-time job, but I don't trust her. She can't seem to trace some of the money I know we had in our business account," Paul said to me one day after work.

"Do you have any proof to back up your suspicions?" I asked.

"No, it's the damndest thing. I can't prove it now that we've been entrusting this job to her for so many months. She claims the funds are low because a few customers are past due on accounts receivable, and we shouldn't be worried," he continued. "But, hell, I'm worried. I think I should get out with whatever money I've invested."

"Well, if it is true, I guess you'd better. I'm so sorry it had to end like this, Paul. You and Jim worked so hard and put so many hours into this new company. But it would be hard to challenge Jim's wife without him taking offense. If you get out now, at least you wouldn't risk losing even more," I added.

It seemed a shame it had to come to an end when the new business was just starting to gain momentum. But again, it wasn't my life or career. Paul needed to do what he felt was right. The disturbing part was watching him become disenchanted with more and more things. But at least he had kept his promise to me. He hadn't used alcohol in two years. I hadn't seen him drink, nor had I smelled alcohol on his breath. When we socialized, he requested Diet Cokes and so did I. I figured my not using alcohol was a small price to pay to keep our marriage on an even keel.

Granted, I was not head over heels in love with Paul like I had been earlier in our marriage. He was rarely emotionally available to me as far as confiding and sharing his inner most thoughts and feelings. Any attempts to ask about how he was feeling were viewed as my attempts to be his "shrink." I stopped asking, but kept open to listening. It was essential to keep very firm boundaries around my professional life and not allow any obvious "seepage" from psychology or psychotherapy to contaminate our marriage. I decided I could live without emotional intimacy since he was not comfortable with any personal sharing. As long as we could provide a stable and loving home for the kids, I would survive. Once the kids were grown, I'd revisit our relationship issues. But for now, the wheels were in motion. I wanted to give our kids the best future I possibly could. As long as Paul was going in the same general direction, I'd be all right.

So in early 1985, Paul decided to embrace new career paths. He became a vocational counselor in rehabilitation hospitals and a farm appraiser. The counseling endeavor was an outgrowth of his master's degree in industrial technology. His farm appraiser status grew out of his license as a realtor. I was happy about his versatility. He certainly had a variety of credentials to pull himself out of any fires he found himself in; sometimes, fires he'd created.

We had also inherited farm acreage, along with Paul's siblings, after his parents passed away. We decided to extract ourselves from this group ownership and use the proceeds to purchase our own eighty-acre farm. This seemed like a good decision, since the new farm paid for itself. We made our farm and tax payments from the corn and soybeans we sold. There were many farmers for hire to help sow and harvest. Paul even liked to do the farm work himself when he had the time. He said he got "itchy" to be on a tractor when spring rolled around.

Paul eventually did well enough to purchase another seventy acres in another county.

One day after work, Paul and I were standing in the kitchen getting dinner ready while the kids kicked a soccer ball around outside. Paul poured himself a Diet Coke and said, "It would be nice to leave Ann and Max their own farms when we die," he explained.

"Yes, it would," I agreed. "As long as we can help them with college when the time comes," I added.

"Of course we can. Haven't I done well with real estate and farm acquisitions so far?" he asked.

"Yes, you have. It's been working quite well." And I thought to myself it was all because he hadn't been drinking.

I'm not sure of the exact time Paul began acting paranoid about our local police, but one day he said, "The cops are harassing me, because my Toyota truck has a few miles on it and some visible rust. They can't handle rust in this upscale town. I'm not exactly the "poster boy" for such an affluent community. Sometimes they actually follow me around," he claimed.

"I don't think we have the only rusty truck in town. I can't imagine the police have time to follow you around when there are actual crimes being committed," I reasoned.

"OK, then explain this. Yesterday when I was driving home from the farm, a couple of cops started following me for no apparent reason, and I had to drive like hell to get away from them."

"You tried to outrun them?"

"Damn right. I know all the back roads out in the country, so don't worry. I clocked about 110 miles an hour at one point. The old truck might be rusty, but it can go like hell. The cops will never catch me," he boasted.

I looked around downstairs to make sure the kids weren't within earshot. I was grateful they were upstairs. His grandiosity seemed like that of an alcoholic, but he hadn't been drinking. I smelled no alcohol on him and his eyes and his speech looked normal. Again, I wondered if he could have bipolar disorder. He also had a lot of symptoms for ADD/ADHD although he'd never been diagnosed as a child. If he had ADD/ADHD co-occurring with bipolar disorder, the symptoms could be intensified. Or could I have missed his drinking on occasion and I should consider the possibility of comorbidity with alcohol abuse? I had a quick fantasy of slipping a little lithium in his coffee to see what effect it would have.

I'd never get Paul in to see a psychiatrist voluntarily, and he hadn't done anything severe enough to warrant an involuntary hospitalization. He hadn't done anything verifiable yet, nor had he been caught doing anything illegal or dangerous. It would be my word versus his word. He was a vocational therapist with no current job difficulties. I was a psychotherapist. He had resisted my prior suggestions about needing marital counseling, a sleep study or A.A. He was convinced he needed no professional help and wished I would stop being a "shrink" for awhile. I was adhering to the rule of therapists not practicing on my own family members, but I wished I could get him in the door to see someone else.

Paul's behavior appeared manic or at the least, hypomanic. Irritability was present through both depressive and manic episodes. One day we heard sad news about a former classmate of ours. He was also Ann's godfather. Paul and I liked him and his wife a lot. On the afternoon that Paul learned of Rich's finger and thumb amputation due to cancer, it triggered an acute depressive episode. He began drinking again after what I believed was an absence of drinking for many years.

He sat on the raised hearth of our fireplace. "Life is useless. What the hell's the point?" he said.

I tried to comfort him. "This is terrible news about Rich, but he'll come through it. He's a fighter and has a very supportive family. I know he'll survive this."

"How in the love of God can you stand there and say that? My parents didn't come through. Your mom didn't come through. Everyone I've ever loved and cared about has died. I don't see much point in going on," he added.

"Paul, you're scaring me. You don't plan to do anything to hurt yourself do you? If you are, I'll call the police to take you straight to the hospital. This is serious," I said.

"No, now don't get excited. I'll be fine if you leave me alone. You worry too much. I need to be by myself right now. Get out of here."

I went upstairs, but not far away. I knelt down and prayed. I wasn't sure what else to do. I called Pastor Greg and asked him if he could help me and talk with Paul and urge him to see a doctor. Paul liked and respected Pastor Greg. He had some credibility.

I went downstairs, got my keys and drove about a mile north up the road from our house to meet him. "Thanks for seeing me on such short notice. I'm really worried about Paul, but I need your support to get him some professional help," I said.

Our entire family loved Pastor Greg. He was a bit younger than Paul, but very sincere and hard-working. He was a very good man and a committed Christian.

After sharing my concerns about Paul, Pastor Greg said, "Carol, I'd prefer not to get involved. I'll pray for Paul, but you know he's on our church council and he's really doing a good job. I don't see any of these inappropriate or alarming behaviors you describe."

"With all due respect, Pastor, you don't live with him. He is on his best behavior when he's at a council meeting. It is when he's with me, the kids, or even alone that I worry about him. Other situations have caused me concern," I added. Pastor looked at me strangely, and I had a vague feeling he was looking at me as though I was mentally unstable.

"I'm sure you have some valid concerns. If I notice anything amiss with Paul the next time I see him, I'll get back to you. In the meantime, I will pray for him," he said.

"Pastor, I hope he's still around for the next council meeting. He needs professional help and he respects you. He doesn't value my opinion as a professional now. He may listen to you."

My pleadings fell on deaf ears. I left feeling sad and hopeless.

Even if I could arrange an involuntary hospitalization, Paul wouldn't be kept long enough. I had seen some of my clients with serious suicidal ideation released only after forty-eight hours. I had helped hospitalize an adolescent boy who had a specific plan and means to carry out his suicide the week before. He was released in forty-eight hours after he convinced everyone on the hospital staff that he was emotionally stable. I felt very uneasy about the decision, but my concerns were overridden by the staff. I knew Paul could fake wellness to get released. He could still pull himself together if it served his own interests. He'd really impressed Pastor Greg.

CHAPTER 11

The MG

In a few days, this depressive episode subsided and Paul began a new project. He decided to order a convertible MG kit car.

"It will be fun. I've always wanted an MG," he said.

He showed me the photos in a glossy brochure and I agreed the finished vehicle looked beautiful. Parts soon started arriving at our home. He needed an engine and transmission from another car before he could dive into this new project. He bought a fifteen-year-old rusted Ford Pinto and parked it in front of our house at the bottom of the hill. It seemed to generate discussion as the neighbors walked past our house. They may have looked askance, but no one complained to us directly. The rusty car did nothing to enhance our home's "curb appeal." Paul soon tore out the Pinto engine and strung it on pulleys in our two-car garage. Everything we had stored in the garage was squeezed to the side. We no longer had room to park either car in the garage. I started to resent the project when we had to scrape ice and shovel snow to free our cars before going to work. For several years, I looked at the ugly car parked out in front of our home. The neighbors were too polite to say anything directly, but I'm sure they weren't pleased. "You'll have to get used to this minor inconvenience until my project is finished," Paul said.

"I find it more than a little inconvenient, Paul. I rush around enough in the morning, getting the kids ready for school without having to chisel out a car encrusted in snow and ice. It is really a huge inconvenience, not minor at all."

"Don't worry, Carol. Once this car is done, you'll love it and it will all have been worth it," he said.

"So, when do you think it might be done?" I asked.

"Depends on how much time I have."

I had serious doubts about this project, especially with no tentative completion date.

At the same time this major project was under way, Paul began filling our basement with "collectibles" as he transformed our basement into a recreation room. This had seemed like a suburban ritual to me. Many of our neighbors had already been through this. It was always capped by a neighborhood party for the basement "unveiling." If this were Paul's only major project, I wouldn't have been overly concerned, but he wanted it to coincide with the MG construction project.

One evening as I prepared one more easy casserole for dinner, Paul trudged into the kitchen hauling a bundle of things I'd never seen before. He stomped the snow off his boots and held up an old barrel with rusty metal trim.

"Hey, look at what I found," he said.

"Mmm … it looks like an old barrel," I said stating the obvious.

"You're damn right. It's a honey, isn't it? I figured we'd need this when the basement is finished. It would be nice to set things on."

"Well, I guess … "

"And that's not all I found at this garage sale. Look at this old horse collar. I can see this on a wall downstairs. It'll really add to the atmosphere. I couldn't pass it up," he added.

"I wasn't sure what theme we'd chosen for the basement. It sounds like you'd like a rustic, country or Western theme," I said.

"Yeah, I think that would be really cool. Do you like it?"

"Yeah, I could see that, but I wish we could talk through our ideas first before you go shopping for decorating items," I said.

"I know, but I really liked these things, so I took a chance. But I've saved the best for last."

Paul reached into a brown paper bag and brought out an old moth-eaten coat made of horsehair.

"Do you have any idea what this is?" he asked.

"Well, off the top of my head, it looks like a shabby old coat," I said, a little sarcastic.

"It's not merely an old coat. It's an antique Indian coat, one of a kind. A vintage coat circa 1850. I'm sure the history museum in the city will pay me thousands of dollars for it."

I'm not sure why I glanced out our dining room window toward our driveway, but I did and gasped. I glimpsed the back of the pickup truck brimming with an assortment of "stuff." I wasn't sure what the stuff was, but the truck was piled high with it.

"Paul, it looks like you found a lot of good buys from what I can see in the back of the truck."

"I sure did. I hit the bonanza today. It will take me a long time to show you everything. But in the meantime, I'm going to start unloading the truck and sort through my new treasures out in the garage," Paul said. He spoke rapidly and raced from describing one found item to the next.

Paul's paycheck was smaller than it once was, and it had been a long time since his last real estate commission. I was feeling anxious.

"Paul, I know you think we needed all of these treasures, but I hope they didn't cost a lot. Our mortgage is due by the end of the week and we received Ann's new orthodontist bill in the mail today ..."

Paul interrupted me. "Stop worrying. This didn't set us back more than a couple hundred bucks, and it's all good stuff we needed to renovate the basement," he countered.

Over the last few months, I'd noticed more projects being initiated but fewer reaching completion. They all stalled for a variety of reasons. I saw the train coming down the track, but felt helpless to stop it.

Paul carted so much stuff downstairs that evening, I was dismayed. There was no longer room to walk. We'd run out of room for the kids to play in the basement. Much of what Paul brought in was broken, battered and old. They weren't the antiques he used to find that could be refinished and made beautiful with a little elbow grease. It was all garbage. I felt a surge of anger.

When Paul fell asleep on the sofa in front of a roaring fire that night, I tiptoed downstairs and began throwing things in the fire. He didn't move. He never saw me. I felt no guilt. I felt some satisfaction in releasing my anger. I was tired of being ignored. I knew this was passive aggressive, but I had no other way to express my rage and stay married. Paul never missed or even noticed the things I had burned. He had filled a truck with more things than he could remember.

CHAPTER 12

Where Did that Truck Come from and Other Questions (Six Months Later)

I loved spring. We were past the crocuses, daffodils and tulips, but I had lilacs in several vases filling the air with their beautiful scent. Our yard was so pretty with peonies, hyacinths and two cherry trees in bloom. The Ginkgo tree and the red maple were growing rapidly. I loved to see the things we'd planted flourishing.

But not everything in my life was flourishing. A surprise for me tarnished the beauty of spring. Paul came home in a mint green pickup truck right before dinner one evening. The truck looked about thirty years old and displayed more rust than green paint.

When he came in the door, I said, "So, where did the truck come from?"

"It was parked near our farm. It's been there for months. I'm not sure who it belongs to, so I drove it home."

"You drove home a truck belonging to someone else?" He sounded so matter-of-fact and I was thinking he's about to be arrested.

"Yeah, no big deal. I'll use it for a few days and then take it back where I found it. Don't worry. I'm not stealing it or anything. I'll borrow it for a few days," he added.

"Well, I can't say I like the idea. It looks like a road hazard and it belongs to someone we don't even know. I think it should go back where you found it immediately," I said.

I expected him to be irritated.

"I have a bigger concern right now," he continued. "Do you see these boots? Can you tell I've been in a fire?" I looked down and saw he was wearing a pair of scorched boots. "Yes, they look charred and crispy." I decided to try humor. "Looks like you went to a barbecue and your boots were the entrée," I laughed.

"It's not funny. I had to start a brush fire out at the farm and it got a little out of hand. I burned both boots, but the left one's the worst. It got a little warm under there, but I stomped it out before the fire went clear through to me. I got lucky," he said.

"You sure did. I'm glad you're all right. Boots can always be replaced, unlike toes. I'm still thinking about the truck, but I know you're not concerned. Your borrowing a truck without the owner's knowledge sounds like stealing to me. Don't you think you need to return it before he knows it's missing?"

"No problem. I have lots to do at the farm. I'll be going there a lot in the next few days," he said.

"Good," I said. It was bad enough we had a rusted Pinto in front of our house. We really didn't need a clunker truck out in our driveway, too.

The best part of the day was listening to a red cardinal sing in one of the oak trees. I stopped washing pots and pans long enough to enjoy his song through the open kitchen window and watch the ivory Battenberg lace curtains flutter.

CHAPTER 13

Fear

The following year in 1984, I accepted a new position. Ann was now in 7th grade and Max was in 2nd grade. Since they were enrolled full time in school, I thought I could try a new job whose hours conformed to their school day. I decided to work for our county's truancy prevention program and assist in trying to return truants to school. Although I embraced the mission of the project, I underestimated the danger factor.

My position consisted of trying to keep parents and kids out of court by returning students to school and maintaining regular attendance. I visited families in their homes in two counties and attended school conferences and court once or more per week. We worked with the assistant district attorney to put pressure on the parents and sometimes the students to return to school.

I found working with the homeless and underprivileged very challenging. I worked with families who had been impacted by violent crimes and physical and sexual abuse. Some students were members of street gangs and many were addicted to alcohol and other drugs. Some were members of satanic cults. I received a police escort about five times in my six years of employment. I was threatened with knives, guns and bombs. I sometimes saw children who bore the signs of physical abuse or gross neglect. I often had to call the child abuse hotline to report what I had witnessed. As a family therapist, I was a mandated reporter concerning my suspicions of abuse or neglect. It was physically and emotionally draining. I became extra protective of my own children after viewing the calamities and chaos I witnessed each day.

Nevertheless, I enjoyed my job. I liked the other professionals I worked with, with few exceptions. I enjoyed seeing kids get back in school who hadn't been attending for a long time. We saw our mission as helping children achieve brighter futures and hopefully decreasing the dropout rate. We provided families with resources, so if there were financial, health, abuse or housing issues interfering with school attendance, we could guide them to the appropriate agencies.

In May of 1988, I was looking forward to the end of another school year and wrapping up my cases with the county. I had worked in the program for four years and had also started an evening private practice, counseling two nights a week.

It was a beautiful spring day and flowers were blooming again. I was looking forward to celebrating my father's 73rd birthday that evening. Paul had suggested we go to dinner with my dad and stepmother in my hometown where they still lived, slightly over an hour away from our home.

About mid-afternoon, Paul started trimming bushes in our backyard. He decided to trim not only ours, but two other neighbors' yards as well. Our next door neighbors were away, so Paul mowed the far side of their lot facing the street to help them out while they were gone. The neighbor adjacent to their yard was a brittle diabetic and had a hard time doing yard work, so Paul sometimes helped him mow the back section of his yard. This was a thoughtful gesture on Paul's part, though not well-timed. As it got later, I reminded Paul of our dinner date and told him we'd need to leave in about an hour if we were to be on time for the reservation we'd made. He became extremely angry and threw down his gardening tools. This dinner engagement had been his idea a month ago, so I wasn't sure why he was upset now. He marched inside the kitchen and said. "I'm taking a shower. Get the kids in the car."

"All right." I answered.

He was dressed and in the car in fifteen minutes. We drove from our neighborhood through the rural area we traveled so often between our homes. Paul loved traveling the back roads in the country.

"Fewer cops," he said.

"Paul, the speedometer says 90. Please slow down. It'll be all right if we're a little late. I'd rather we arrive late than not at all."

"If getting there on time is so damned important, I'll get us there on time."

The kids looked frightened, and I was frightened. He started driving erratically on purpose, delighting in our fear.

"Paul, stop the car. Let us out. If you can't drive safely and slow down, I want out now and the kids will come with me."

He ignored me. I restated my case to no avail. It didn't matter what I said or how I asked, he ignored me.

By the time we reached the restaurant to meet my parents, my festive mood had changed to one of pure relief. We had arrived safely. The kids looked relieved, too. If I'd given myself the risk-of-harm inventory I gave my female clients, I'd have a pretty high score. However, knowing I worked with women in far more dangerous situations than mine, I would be all right, and so would the kids.

CHAPTER 14

Christmas in Cuernavaca

One day in the fall of 1988, Paul came home from work and told me he'd been thinking about the upcoming holidays.

"You know, I've been thinking we might want to do something different for Christmas this year."

"Like what?" I asked.

"I don't want another one with the relatives like last year. It's such a hassle with travel, bad weather, all of the gifts and exchanging things no one ever seems to want or need. I hate the ordeal of drawing names or buying for everyone. No one seems to like our suggestions, so why not do something different?"

"I'm ready for a change, too. What are you thinking about?"

"Well, I picked up a travel guide at the bookstore called *Fodor's Mexico*. I've always wanted to go there and he tells you the best way to see it. Ann is in her third year of Spanish in high school. She could probably be very helpful as our translator," he said.

"Would we fly there and rent a car?"

"Yeah. We'd have Christmas here at home and the kids could open the envelope with our plane tickets under the tree. We'd fly out the next day. They would be so surprised."

"You're right, they sure would."

I was surprised by this idea, but drawn to something so out of the ordinary. I was sure the kids would love the plan. I began to secretly look through Fodor's book when the kids weren't around. There would be so many interesting things to do and see in Mexico. It would be hard to narrow it down with only ten days of travel.

By the time Christmas Day arrived I was as excited as the kids. Ann and Max emptied their stockings by the fireplace while Christmas carols played in the background. Paul and I sipped our coffee waking up to the level of the kids' excitement.

Next we all went to the living room to begin opening the gifts under the tree. There weren't as many items under the tree this year, and Paul and I knew why. The kids would understand in a few minutes. We told them to open the big gifts first. The suspense was building. They both loved the gifts they received, but we saved the best until last. Ann and Max carefully opened the envelope together. At first they didn't understand what the four tickets meant. Ann held them up to read more closely and read the words *Mexico City* and let out a big war whoop. She and Max hugged each other and shouted with joy. It was exactly the effect Paul and I had hoped for. Oh, this would be such fun.

The first thing I remember about Mexico City was the smell of burning garbage. We had landed safely and paid for our rental car. It was late at night when we arrived, so we couldn't see much of the city, but the smell of garbage burning was overwhelming. When we arrived at the hotel we had booked, our credit card reservation had somehow not been recorded properly. The hotel had no record of Paul's reservation. After much haggling, Paul was able to negotiate a room on the thirteenth floor. The room was adequate, but not spectacular. The biggest problem was the lack of water pressure. Somehow the water didn't make it to the top floors of the hotel. The shower emitted a few drops of water and then dried up completely. We decided to get another hotel for the following night. There were plenty of better places to stay in such a big city.

All four of us loved Mexican food, but we were unaccustomed to service "Mexico style." At the first four restaurants we visited, our family was served with ten -minute intervals between each person. We were used to everyone in the family being served at the same time. I was amazed at Paul's patience with this, but at the fifth restaurant, he became visibly irritated.

"Why," Paul asked the waiter, "does it seem so difficult to serve our entire family at the same time?"

"Sir," the waiter explained patiently, "can I help it if the chef is drunk in the kitchen?"

"No, I suppose you can't," answered Paul.

I hid my chuckle. I wondered how Paul liked being inconvenienced by someone else's drinking.

In addition to the noxious smell of garbage was the high visibility of Mexican soldiers with machine guns. Pickup trucks filled with armed guards drove through the city. Whenever we had to get gas and use the restrooms at the Pemex stations, we had to pass an armed guard in front of the restroom. When we entered jewelry stores, I told the kids to be very careful not to touch anything, since there were armed guards present in each store. It wasn't until we returned to the states that we read about the failed coup attempted in Mexico over the holidays.

On the second day of our stay in Mexico City, I decided I would travel without my purse and documents in order to reduce the risk of being pick-pocketed. As we got on the crowded subway, everyone managed to board but me—I was left behind. I didn't speak Spanish and had no ID or money. I found an official- looking guard and asked him if he spoke English. Thankfully he did. He suggested I board again and go to the next stop; he thought I'd find my family waiting. I did as he suggested and they were there, except for Ann. She had gone back alone to find me. Now I was really frightened. Paul, Max and I got back on the subway and went back to our original stop and there was Ann. I said my prayers of thanksgiving. What a miracle. I was tired of the city and longed for home, but our adventure had just begun.

Our trip had started out less relaxing than anticipated. Things were bound to get better. Our plan was to drive to Cuernavaca, then Taxco and finally Acapulco. We foundered on our way to Cuernavaca. It was 9:00 p.m. and we were traveling in circles through destitute little towns that all looked the same. I was getting frightened about being lost in a strange land. The kids had both fallen asleep, for which I was grateful. I didn't want them to be as frightened as I was.

We pulled in front of a lighted building so we could review the Fodor map. Our car was immediately surrounded by large barking German Shepherds, and I saw a large group of uniformed men approaching us. They were obviously policemen. We didn't want police attention in Mexico, but maybe they could help us find our way to Cuernavaca. The barking dogs woke up the kids. An officer appeared at the side of Ann's window as she was yawning. I asked her to quickly think about how to tell the officer we were lost in Spanish. Ann was barely awake, let alone up to speed with her Spanish vocabulary, but managed to string a sentence together which was more than the rest of us could do. I heard lots of men talking in response to Ann, all at the same time.

"They said they would help us find Cuernavaca. We just have to follow behind them, Dad," said Ann.

We followed a police car filled with six officers. The lights were flashing on their squad car and I envisioned them taking us to a Mexican jail and never being heard from again. I was terrified when I realized they were toying with us. They drove around the same block over and over. We were afraid to leave them, but we were not going to make progress driving around in a circle. I could see the silhouettes of the men in front of us and I could tell they were all laughing and thinking this was great sport. I wondered how long the game would continue. We were all so very tired. It was two hours later when the driver got out of the car and simply pointed at a road on our right. We took this signal to mean they were done with us and to depart. We all breathed a sigh of relief when we saw the words Cuernavaca on a sign up ahead.

We found an old hotel that had a vacancy light on. It looked pretty bad from the outside, but at this hour we couldn't be choosy. Again, Ann helped us arrange to stay the night. Her limited Spanish skills got us through again. We enjoyed the sights and sounds of the town the next day. It was a good visit with shops and restaurants.

Next we were off to Taxco, the silver capital of Mexico. We found the city filled with tents, where silver jewelry was being sold at a fraction of the price back home. We bought gifts for friends and relatives and delighted in the bargains. In sad contrast, it was disturbing to see extreme poverty and many dead burros on the sides of the roads as we traveled. We weren't used to seeing that back home.

Acapulco was our next and last stop before our return journey. The city was unfortunately populated with many homeless street people who begged and grabbed at our pockets. Paul had made the mistake of giving the children candy and money at first, but showed total irritation with them when he acquired a following like the Pied Piper. We decided to get off the streets and head for the beach. We rented a charter fishing boat and Paul and Max were each able to catch a giant sailfish by the end of the day. Max's fish was over nine feet long, so we decided to have it stuffed. He was so proud to have caught such a huge fish at the age of twelve. Shipping it back to the states was the most expensive part of that venture. We donated Paul's fish to the poor.

The following day, we decided to go for a swim in the Pacific. It was a perfect morning for strolling on the beach and watching the parasailing antics of the tourists. Paul, Ann and Max were about a hundred yards ahead of me while I lagged behind looking for seashells. My head was down, focused on seashells when I finally looked up to see a giant wave unlike any I had ever seen. It was headed our way, but my family was unaware and the noise on the beach combined with the roar of the ocean covered my screams to "Watch out!" Within seconds, Ann was washed out to sea with Paul jumping in after her. I ran to catch up to them and found Max safe on the shore. Paul came back carrying Ann in his arms. The top of her swimsuit had disappeared and she lied limp in his arms. Her pretty ceramic earrings had been ripped from her ears. I wasn't sure if she was alive or dead. Paul gently laid her down on the ground. She wasn't breathing. I tried to push water out of her lungs. Some water started gurgling out of her mouth. We were surrounded by soldiers in uniform who pointed their long guns at us and watched curiously. We could have used the help of a lifeguard, not an armed soldier. Finally, Ann sputtered and coughed and sputtered again. Slowly she became conscious again, and I thanked God.

"I have a headache," she complained.

"We're so glad that's all that's wrong. You were knocked out by an enormous wave. I'd never seen a wall of water quite so high!" I said.

Paul volunteered to track down some aspirin. He was offered cocaine several times on the street, but found it more difficult to find a pharmacy where he could get aspirin. We decided Acapulco would look better from our rearview mirror. Home was sounding comforting after this vacation. I thought this might be the real benefit of the vacation. Perhaps I could return home and be less upset about Paul's behavior.

Our last meal in Acapulco became memorable for all of the wrong reasons. We visited a Big Boy hamburger drive in. The system for ordering was a little confusing, and not due to the language barriers. The customer entered one line to place an order. A few minutes later, the customer was called by number and stood in another line to pick up the order. After waiting for more than a half hour, Paul went to the order line to find out the problem. He had never been given a written receipt or written number and they acted as though he hadn't paid for the food. Paul had paid, but they had told him to remember his number without anything given in writing. Paul was angry, justifiably so, and he threatened to call the police. They also threatened to call the police. I urged Paul to forget the $15.00 and we could go elsewhere for lunch. It wasn't worth a fight. But Paul was not one to give in easily and continued to block the flow of customers. My stomach was in knots, and the kids were embarrassed and worried about Paul. It took another half hour, but eventually we were served. I was very ready to go home.

After we returned to the states, I decided that Paul wasn't really that symptomatic. Most anyone would have been upset with the unsatisfactory service at the fast food restaurant.

CHAPTER 15

An Old Rag

One day in October of 1989, Paul announced we would need to sell our second farm at a $70,000 loss. This was significant, because I was earning about $25,000 with my new contract with the county. Paul was earning about the same as a vocational therapist. The farm had been paying for itself. By the time we paid the taxes, the bank, the seed and fertilizer bill and our tenant to farm it, it was a break-even proposition rather than a profitable one. But we knew the farm would increase in value over the years if we could hold onto it. We had been willing to make sacrifices in the present in order to keep a good investment alive. I bought clothing on sale and tried to manage our money carefully to make it work out. Now I was astonished and horrified. How could this be?

"The price of corn and soybeans has taken a hit the last couple of years. I've found a buyer for the farm. If we hold onto it any longer, we could suffer even greater losses. In other words, we'll lose our ass," he said.

I suddenly remembered cutting out those grocery store coupons over the years, carefully trying to make our modest incomes cover the monthly expenses. And now I was being told the offer for our farm was $70,000 less than what we paid for it five years before.

"Paul, I never heard a hint from you that we might be in trouble. I'm angry. That money was going to help us pay for the kids' college tuition someday. I can't believe it's over. Are you sure we need to take the offer as it stands? Couldn't we find another buyer?" I asked.

"I'm afraid not," he added. "Times are hard for farmers now. We'd be lucky to keep this buyer. I think we have no choice but to take it."

I felt sick and angry. My prior trust in Paul's financial plans now waivered.

I had a suicidal fantasy about crashing my car into a tree or utility pole, if only I could make it look like an accident. Maybe then the kids could get my life insurance money to pay for college. But my conscience kicked in and I realized I could never do that. I would never leave Ann and Max to cope with life without me.

In January of 1990, I started a new position as a prevention coordinator for seven school districts. I had been covering seventeen school districts in two counties, and so the scope of this job was appealing. I would also have an office and not need to travel many miles each day. A fifteen -mile commute each way was a definite improvement. I had been driving as much as one hundred miles a day.

The title "prevention coordinator" seemed ironic. I certainly hadn't been successful at preventing a lot of things in my own life. However, I did believe that helping kids make decisions to avoid using alcohol and other drugs made sense. No matter how great life's problems, I was convinced the kids who turned to alcohol and other drugs to escape reality would cease to grow emotionally and risk their health, school future and sometimes their very life. This position sounded much safer. I was tired of being threatened with weapons in public housing projects. I was tired of not having any police protection except in the most extreme situations. Overall, this job sounded much better.

My hours were compatible with the kids' school day. I wasn't always home when they arrived, but it wasn't too much later. It was no worse than my county job as far as the hours went. One day when I came home from work, I noticed I'd gotten a stain on my new blue chambray dress from *Banana Republic*, a slight but rare splurge for my new job. I took the dress down to the workbench in the basement where Paul had various projects gathered together, the latest being antique brass scales. I moved some scales out of the way and started to apply stain remover to the dress when the phone rang. I ran upstairs to answer it and then got preoccupied with starting dinner. I intended to finish working on my dress after we finished eating, but instead I helped the kids with their homework and didn't have time to get back to my dress until the next day.

I went downstairs and found my dress where I had left it, cut in little pieces in a pile. I was stunned. I looked for Paul.

"Paul, do you know what happened to my new dress?" I asked. "It's cut into little pieces."

"Oh, that … I thought it was an old rag, so I cut it up with the lawn clippers," he said.

"Did you *look* at it? How could you mistake a new dress for an old rag?" I was incredulous.

"I don't know," he said and walked away. I followed him.

"Paul, I'm worried about you. Most people wouldn't mistake a new dress for a rag. I think you need help. The dress was a bit of a splurge for my new job. We can't afford to buy new clothes and then cut them up!" I sounded hysterical. My voice was pitched higher and louder than usual.

"Yeah," Paul said and walked away again.

All night I wondered why I was still married to him. I still loved him, but sometimes I felt pity, even hatred. Sometimes I cried myself to sleep. I didn't believe in divorce except for very grave reasons. Paul wasn't having an affair. I imagined an attorney asking me why I wanted a divorce. Could I say that it was because my husband acted strangely at times and even cut up my new dress? Could I say he went over the speed limit on the country roads and frightened me and the kids? Could I say I didn't like what he purchased at garage sales and I thought his finds were all a waste of money?

Were these reasons enough to get a divorce and reduce the kids' access to their dad? He loved them. He made them laugh, helped them with their homework and built them a fantastic gym set in the backyard. He grilled out and made the best fish sauce in the world. He took on projects around the house. He wallpapered, made crown molding and fixed most anything. They still adored their father, despite his occasional odd behavior. But this marriage I constructed in my mind was fiction.

Was I staying married because of my fear of being alone?

My stepmother said, "It's better to be alone than to wish you were." Sometimes I did wish I were alone, but I would feel so much guilt if I divorced prematurely. I decided that I would have a sense of clarity if it got bad enough. I didn't feel the time had come yet.

A little over a year later, in April of 1991, Paul told me he wanted to buy another farm. I was shocked.

"Paul, we're recovering from the sale of our other farm, which was a heart -stopping loss for us. How can we do this? We've been trying to recover from our mistake for quite awhile. Why would you consider another farm?" I asked.

"Corn and bean prices are better now and this farm is a fantastic opportunity. It's a bargain and it won't stay on the market long. I know a guy who'll rent it for us and it won't cost much per acre. I'm serious. I don't think we can afford to pass this up," he said. He spread out maps of the property on our kitchen table.

Looking down at the maps, I said, "Maybe if we hadn't gone through such a loss a short time ago, I'd be more excited about this new opportunity, but now I'm very reluctant. I know you think the farm can pay for itself, Paul, but we have no control over so many variables: the price of corn and beans, the weather, the price of fertilizer ... "

I didn't get to continue. Paul curled up the maps and walked out to the garage. My reluctance had angered him. I didn't care. I wasn't about to give a nod to a major purchase I didn't believe in. I didn't want a repeat of our previous disaster. What was he thinking? I was glad he was going on a church fishing trip that weekend. Perhaps he'd discuss his plan with the guys and they'd talk him out of it.

CHAPTER 16

Ring of Fire

Paul returned from his fishing trip in an excellent mood. I thought it was good that he had gotten away and had a break in his routine to enjoy life and get away from work. He was laughing again for the first time in months.

"So, what did you enjoy the most during the weekend with your buddies?" I asked.

"Laughing at Gavin, that wimp," he said.

"Why was Gavin a wimp? He's always seemed nice to me, outgoing and friendly," I offered.

"Well, he fell asleep after a few drinks on the beach. Maybe he passed out. I'm not sure. But anyway, I dug a shallow trench around him in the sand with my foot. Then I poured gasoline in the trench and lit a match until the flames engulfed him. He was scared out of his wits. We were all standing around him, laughing. Gavin had no sense of humor whatsoever," he added.

"Paul, I can't believe someone didn't call the police. That sounds like a criminal act to me. That's horrific! How did Gavin get out of the circle of fire?"

"Oh, after awhile we all doused the fire with water and he walked off. He wasn't hurt at all. He drove home early. He was pretty pissed."

"I'll be surprised if he doesn't bring charges against you and the other guys who were a part of this prank."

This story haunted me. I wasn't satisfied with Paul's explanation. Maybe Paul had started drinking and made this up. Could it have really happened like he described? I made phone calls to several of the men who had gone on the trip. They all stuck together in their versions of Paul's story. It had only been a "prank." Paul hadn't meant any harm. He was trying to get a few laughs. They all thought it was funny.

I talked to Pastor Greg. He agreed with the other men.

"Gavin is being ultra sensitive. He's leaving our church. Paul meant no harm by it," said Pastor Greg.

Was I the only one who thought this was criminal? This was crazy behavior in my eyes. If a person is on church council, does he have certain immunity from consequences?

CHAPTER 17

Mr. Hyde Wore Silver Nitrate

Ann turned nineteen the following month. It seemed like yesterday she was an infant in my arms. Now she was taking college courses. Where did the time go?

Sometime in November, after the first snowfall of 1991, Paul decided it would be fun to go snowmobiling up north with Max before his sixteenth birthday. I ignored my misgivings, clung to my fantasies and focused on their mutual love of snowmobiling. They headed north after Max got home from school and decided to rent snowmobiles once they got up there rather than dragging our own. On Saturday night, I got a call from Max.

"Mom, Dad's been in a snowmobile accident, but he doesn't want you to worry and said to tell you he'll be all right. He looks a little scuffed up, though." I could sense Max's attempts to deescalate my alarm, as instructed by his father.

"So Max, how scuffed up is he? Was he drinking?" I asked.

Max answered my question in a roundabout way.

"Well, he was going about seventy miles an hour and flipped the snowmobile up about twelve feet in the air before it landed. His face took the brunt of it, but the more serious injury is his shoulder. We think it might be broken. The doctor in the ER put it in a temporary sling after taking X-rays. He has silver nitrate all over his face and looks sort of scary. He doesn't want you to be alarmed when you first see his face. It should heal. He's in a lot of pain. Oh, and he told me he hadn't been drinking."

"Max, how did your dad get to the ER if he was in so much pain?"

"Well, Mom, he didn't want you to get nervous about this part, either. I drove the truck. But I had to, Mom. And it was all right and I didn't get picked up. I know I don't have my license yet, but I had to get help for Dad. We'll head home in the morning. We'll see you sometime tomorrow night."

"Max, I don't want you driving home, not without a license. You may never get your license if the police stop you."

"Don't worry, Mom. Dad can drive. He said he'll be fine."

"OK, Max. Thanks for preparing me. Now put your dad on the phone. I'd like to talk to him."

There was a long pause.

"Max, are you still there?" I asked.

"Yeah, Mom. I'm here. Dad said he'll talk to you when we get back. He's tired now and needs a good night's rest."

"OK, honey. You tried. Be very careful and call me if you need anything."

"Sure, Mom." My motherly intuition told me those two last words were code for "I can't tell you anything else without making Dad more upset."

When Paul walked through the front door on Sunday night, I didn't recognize him. A grayish cast from the silver -nitrate salve covered most of his face. Clear liquid and tinges of blood seeped through. He looked horrific. He attempted to minimize the situation.

"Hey, I know it looks bad, but it'll be all right in a few days," he explained.

"You may need surgery depending on what those x-rays show," I cautioned.

"Nah, it'll be fine. If it were that serious, the ER doc would have recommended that. I'll be fine in a few days. I'll take a little aspirin for the pain and I'll be as good as new."

After several weeks of incredible pain Paul's cousin, a nurse, asked to see Paul's x-rays which had arrived. She said his collarbone appeared broken and he should see a surgeon immediately. I was thankful Paul listened to her.

Surgery was scheduled shortly after his appointment with the surgeon. Paul's health insurance wasn't in force yet since he had changed jobs again. He needed pins inserted and then surgically removed after a few months. He never allowed me to accompany him to the hospital. I left messages with his doctor, asking him to screen him for frontal lobe disorders, traumatic brain injury. If I thought Paul had seemed irrational before, this new head injury seemed to make things even worse. After the snowmobile accident, Paul got used to living on painkillers to deal with the pain. He was often in a foul mood.

Paul had been such a caring, intelligent, creative and sensitive person. Was he a problem drinker, or an alcoholic? Or was he self-medicating bipolar disorder with alcohol? And now, was he suffering from a traumatic brain injury? He was Dr. Jekyll and Mr. Hyde. I never knew from minute to minute who would be walking in the door. I was feeling on edge a lot.

CHAPTER 18

Nothing to Explain

In the summer of the following year, Paul suggested we sell our beautiful home in the subdivision we'd lived in for the past twelve years. He decided we should move to the country and build a home on our newest farm. I felt time was moving on "fast forward," and he was losing touch with reality.

"Paul, why do we need to sell our beautiful home? I can't understand why you would want to leave our lovely neighborhood and all of the good friends we have. I can walk across the street to get to my office. It's taken me a long time to build my practice and I won't just toss it away. And the commute to my school is long enough without moving out to the country. Why do you want this?"

I watched as Paul poured a Diet Coke into a glass with ice. What else had he poured in that glass before I was looking?

"I think we should build a one-story," he said. "We need to prepare a retirement home. I'd like a master bedroom on the first floor and a great room. We should have those features and the low maintenance we have always talked about. I think it would be great if we left suburbia. We could live on our newest farm. You could open a private practice in the country, helping farmers and their families. Your commute will be longer, but you'll be closer to the freeway. You could garden again, can and freeze vegetables again ..."

"Paul, I don't want to do this. The home design itself is not a bad idea, but I don't want to leave the private practice I've built over the last eight years. I am not interested in expanding my commute time, or gardening, canning and freezing vegetables. It's hard enough juggling all I'm doing," I added.

"You'd get used to the country. I hate the crowds, traffic and taxes here. Cops are always on the lookout in case you happen to be speeding. They're always preying on decent citizens who need to get around. This house will need more maintenance in a few years. We'll need a new roof and furnace soon. We need to update our landscaping too," he said.

"I agree with some of your concerns. A lower- maintenance home in a less crowded area has some merit. I could move five or ten miles out, but not as far as you're suggesting, Paul."

"I'm already planning to buy another house that's coming on the market. I'd like to rent it out and hold it for awhile as an investment property. The land it's on will be very valuable in the near future."

Then Paul dropped the bomb. "I've decided to list our house. We're moving, not sure where we'll end up. But we need to go ASAP. We can always build somewhere and maybe rent for awhile when this house sells."

I was aghast. "I must be missing something. You've already made a decision to list this house and buy another one to rent to tenants? And you're not sure where we'll be living? Paul, we still have a son in high school. We need to let him stay in the same school and not disrupt his education. I don't understand the urgency to sell right away and buy another house to rent out. I know you have valuable inside realtor information, but I'm more worried about uprooting Max from his friends and school than our missing a great opportunity. What is going on, Paul?"

"Here, sign this contract to buy the house I want. If you don't sign, I'll proceed without you anyway. I may even forge your signature if you refuse to sign. Remember it takes 'one to buy and two to sell' in our state. I don't need your signature if you want to play 'hardball' with me."

"Paul, I don't get this or understand you. This is such a shift in how we used to work together. I don't feel as though I'm talking to my husband. What is really going on? Can you please explain?"

"Nothing to explain. I'm out of here. I'll be back when we're new homeowners. I think I have a good lead on some tenants. The house will pay for itself. It's on very desirable land. We'll own it a few years and then sell and make a fortune. Our newest farm is working out well and so is our first one. You'll be glad I had the foresight to get this house. For now, trust me."

He slipped out the kitchen door. I heard his truck start and felt my future slipping from my grasp.

A few hours later, Paul returned with documents in hand.

"We are the proud owners of a home out on Hampton Road. I've got a lead on those tenants. In a year or two, when this property is in prime development territory, you will be thanking me," he said.

In a very brief time span, there were too many changes to assimilate. Now we needed to sell our home, move to an apartment, start building a retirement home somewhere, and look for tenants for our new rental property. I had no vote in this. It all felt crazy.

There was a large part of me that thought Paul was losing his mind. I felt bipolar disorder was manifesting itself. But there was another small part of me that took over. It was a little voice that told me to hang onto hope that this could all work out. I was buying into the crazy ideas and actually envisioning them working out. For now, my little hopeful voice silenced my clinical and rational self.

In the meantime, we had to enroll Max in his new high school. He would attend a smaller high school in the district where we would eventually build our retirement home. It wasn't too far from my private practice office. Maybe this could work.

Much later I would find good judgment. Good judgment comes from experience. Experience comes from bad judgment. I had plenty of that.

CHAPTER 19

The Wedding and the Old Farm Schoolhouse

I was so proud of Max. Transferring to a new high school was not an easy thing in sophomore year and he was handling it with grace. He made the football team and really enjoyed it. It didn't hurt he weighed 235 pounds and was over six feet tall. It also made it easier to make new friends.

But there was a glitch. Max's first football game was scheduled the same night of Ann's rehearsal dinner before her wedding to Jason. Max told his coach about the conflict and the coach told Max he'd have to make a decision. Max told me he had only one sister, and since Jason asked him to be his "best man" he would attend the rehearsal dinner and not play in the game. This was not an easy decision, but I couldn't be more proud of Max. His coach was understandably disappointed.

At this point we were still living in "suburbia." I was having a hard time letting go of the family home we'd lived in for twelve years. So many memories …

I climbed the stairs to our master bedroom and looked out the windows to enjoy the view for the last time. It had always thrilled me to look out at the views. I could see forever up there. The leaves hadn't turned their fall colors yet, but there were hints of yellow in the Gingko tree below. As I looked at the red oak beneath me, I thought about the day Ann smashed her nose into it, riding on her flying saucer in the snow. It had ended in a quick trip to the ER. The mullioned windows were open and a slight breeze blew through and felt good. I wanted to freeze time and never leave the comfort of this room and scene outside. I could hear a cardinal singing. The world looked perfect from my window that morning.

The next day Ann married Jason. It was a perfect warm and sunny Labor Day weekend. They were both only twenty years old in 1992. Paul and I had hoped they would wait, but Ann reminded me her Dad and I were only twenty-two when we married. It seemed old enough to us at the time. I wasn't so sure now.

Even though Ann looked beautiful in her wedding dress with her four bridesmaids standing on the front porch in their long raspberry -colored gowns, I felt detached from the beauty. I would miss Ann very much. Paul danced with her at the reception. He never asked me for one dance. I felt unmarried, tired and sad.

Maybe I felt tired from all the wedding planning. Maybe it was getting to me, working two jobs while Paul worked less and less. Maybe I felt helpless and not able to rescue my own family.

When I thought about Max, I avoided thinking about my own situation. Max worked at settling into his new school. It was not an easy adjustment for him, but he did his best to adapt. He has always been well-liked by those who've met him, a gentle, caring soul and deep thinker, laced with an endearing and dry sense of humor. I knew he would be all right.

Our family home sold quickly after we put it on the market. We had accumulated so many belongings in twelve years. Despite frequent garage sales and spring cleanings, I was amazed at how much extra clutter we had to weed through. I was surprised at how many former treasures now looked tacky.

The worst part of the move involved Paul's slowly healing collarbone. He'd been given strict doctor's instructions not to do any heavy lifting after the pin had been removed. Despite my words of caution, Paul insisted on moving a china cabinet in the dining room without assistance from anyone. He felt something crack and knew immediately what he'd done. The prior surgeries had cost us thousands we hadn't budgeted for. I foresaw more pain and suffering in Paul's near future.

We moved into an old renovated, one-room schoolhouse out on acreage that belonged to Paul's younger sister, Janie. She agreed to lease it to us a month at a time until we could find property and build our retirement home. It had some pretty features, including a massive upstairs bedroom for Max with beautiful hardwood floors. Stained glass windows caught the light and refracted it in pretty streams inside the house. The land surrounding it was covered with pines. It helped to focus on these serene qualities whenever I had to venture into the moldy basement. It also helped me tolerate the cramped kitchen.

Paul had always had what I considered a very strong work ethic, a very appealing trait when we had first met as sophomores in high school. He was far more mature than most guys I had met, so much older and wiser than his peers. Initially, the fact that he had been robbed of most of his childhood coping with his father's illness hadn't registered with me as a deficit. His mother had inherited an eighty - acre farm, so Paul borrowed farm equipment from his grandfather and plowed, sowed and harvested with his younger brother's help. He also worked at a gas station on the weekends. In retrospect, what had seemed like a strong work ethic was an understandable compulsion to keep the bills paid. He needed to pay off his father's hospital bills, because the VA had denied benefits. They claimed there was no proof the brain tumor had been caused by the exploding shell that hit his head in Italy during

WWII. Paul's childhood had been saturated with adult responsibilities and he was a classic *parentified child.*

He'd often told me he wanted to retire by age thirty-five. Although I could understand his desire, I also knew how unrealistic it was. He held multiple jobs at this point, so by age forty-five, he was working as a farm appraiser, realtor and vocational therapist at a hospital. He had had two different hospital positions. He complained about *malingerers* but also staff members and administrators. He always believed a better job would come along.

He had been elected to the church council of our mainstream, Protestant mission church. It entailed many volunteer hours, plus stress and sleep deprivation. I sensed a growing dichotomy between our public selves and private selves. My friends often claimed they envied me, my marriage and our great kids. To the outsider we must have looked good. I started to suspect an intruder in our marriage and it wasn't another woman. It might have been vodka. I wondered if he was self-medicating bipolar disorder with vodka. I could never detect alcohol on his breath. Was he suffering from alcoholism? Could he have a dual diagnosis? What was I dealing with? Once in awhile I'd mention my concerns to a therapist friend and she would agree he needed a thorough evaluation. But until he did something beyond the scope of the law with witnesses present, he would never consent to being seen voluntarily. My requests had all been met with denial and refusal.

CHAPTER 20

The Pinnacle and the Pits

In October of 1992, about a month after moving into the schoolhouse, I accepted the nomination to run for President-elect of the state division for my professional organization, but my excitement was short-lived. Paul came home and told me he had somehow forgotten a $20,000 farm payment due last month. He was crying, explaining how he didn't know how all this had happened. I held him close and reassured him we would resolve the crisis. How? I had no idea. But nevertheless, I reassured him things would be all right.

"They're threatening foreclosure on our newest farm if we don't come up with the money in ten days," he said, his voice breaking.

"Paul, do we have the money?" I asked, dreading the answer I suspected.

"How can this be happening? I *thought* we had the money," he exclaimed in disbelief.

"I thought we were in good shape financially. I thought you'd been making our regular payments since we lost our second farm. I guess that is not what happened…."

"We've also got a tax bill coming due soon. I don't understand how this could have happened," he said as he held his head in his hands and massaged his temples.

I hugged him and said, "I don't know how we'll get through this Paul, but we'll have to somehow. We can't let the farm disappear without a fight."

After discussing our options at length, Paul said, "We'll have to arrange for an auction. That's probably the best outcome we can hope for,' he said.

"You think it will sell? For a decent price, so we can pay back what we owe?"

"Yeah, I think it will. I'll contact a farm auction service I know. It'll sell."

"Paul, you've been working overtime and not getting much sleep. I'd like to go with you to see your doctor. He may be able to help you. Things seem unmanageable now, but we can't go on alone. We need to seek out some help." I instantly regretted using the word *help* because it often triggered such an adverse reaction in people, specifically Paul.

"I don't need to see any goddamn doctor. I'm fine except for your nagging. I'll handle this mess and I sure as hell don't need any help from you or anyone else."

The next morning when Paul left for work, I noticed he'd forgotten his briefcase. Did the contents hold clues as to what was going on? I'd been receiving calls from creditors the last two days, and I kept telling them they must be mistaken. We had always paid our credit card statements on time. I opened Paul's briefcase and found it littered with yellow post-it-notes covered with illegible scribbling. Several dozen unopened bills and monthly statements were inside. How long had this been going on? Some were dated months ago. How could I have been so blind? Everything made more sense now. A feeling of dread descended upon me.

I would confront Paul with these unopened and overdue bills. It had been ten years since that fateful holiday dinner, and now I had concrete evidence that Paul needed to see a doctor. I would not be dismissed again. I would insist he seek professional help. I refused to accept excuses that "someone else" was responsible for his current distress. The "someone else" was often me, but he also included the "overzealous cops," "the crazy office manager," "the arrogant college president" or "the ignorant church council members."

The hard part would be finding a time when he was symptom-free. Paul didn't have many symptom-free moments anymore. There were days he was euphoric and disappeared for most of the day and night, or periods when he was depressed and couldn't get out of bed until after I'd left for work. It enabled him to avoid a conversation about what was happening.

The farm went up for auction. There were no bids. I felt sick to my stomach. I sat in the tent that had been set up on our property and felt my stomach churn. Hope was slipping away. Paul and I drove home in silence.

A few days later Paul received an offer. It wasn't the best, but it would get us out from under what we owed. It was all I wanted now. There would be some details to work out, however. I held my breath.

CHAPTER 21

No Smoking Gun, but a Gun

July 20, 1993, was our twenty-fifth wedding anniversary. I couldn't even bring myself to get Paul a card. I felt our relationship was dead. Fear and ongoing crises kept us connected. Whatever mythical dreams Paul wanted me to believe, I could no longer. They had all been built on his mental illness and had no actual basis in reality. My love had truly been blind.

Oddly enough, I heard a cardinal singing today in our front yard. He sat up high in a maple tree. I hoped he had followed me to our new home.

I was still legally married on July 20, 1993. I was still hoping to help Paul and prevent his further self-destruction. It was based on fear, hope and shame. But it was also rooted in the covenant I made to him when we married, for better or worse. Of course, when I was twenty-two and made those vows, I had no idea how bad "worse" could be.

The day went by unnoticed. Neither of us spoke of our twenty-fifth anniversary.

By the next month, we had moved out of the little schoolhouse to an apartment in our former town. Paul's sister was selling the schoolhouse property, and although we had little notice of our need to move, I was happy. The new apartment complex was called Firethorn, which sounded as painful as our current situation, pain on top of pain. My marriage was dead, but not buried.

I helped Max enroll as a junior in his former high school and he seemed glad to be back with his old friends. They were happy to see him and welcomed him with enthusiasm.

By this time I wasn't sure of myself or our marriage. I felt it all slipping away from me. I had no feelings of security or stability. I hadn't had those feelings for many years. I'd been a pretender and it cost me dearly. An undercurrent in my marriage was pulling me down. But whatever happened to Paul and me, our son Max had a right to a good future and the opportunity to go to college. I had tried to help Ann, but the help was partial, at best. I knew she was strong and would make it, despite her father's actions. I knew taking her car away from her was not right. Paul did this about the time Ann married at age twenty. She trusted him and he'd betrayed her. At least our home then had slightly more stability for her than it now had for Max.

Max decided to drop football and join canoe club. He seemed to be making a mature decision. It meant fewer x-rays and resetting his dislocated shoulder. Paul agreed with his decision. Amazing. I was pleased Max could graduate from the high school he started in.

We decided to stay in the apartment at Firethorn while we worked on finding a lot for our retirement home. I couldn't picture our retirement together, but Paul was working on making blueprints for our home in the country.

Paul had never received a DUI in his life, but he was charged with one in April of 1994. Not only was he charged with a DUI, but four additional charges. He was initially sent to a hospital and then to county jail. He didn't tell me about it until he was home again. Paul traveled so much for work at this point that I hadn't missed him for the two days he was gone. He always seemed to be out of town on real estate ventures.

I often accepted his stories at face value, a habit built on many years of trusting without questioning. But this time I decided to pick up a newspaper to verify his story. I noticed a discrepancy with the timeline Paul had given me. I also found a police report and ambulance bill in a stack of opened mail.

"Paul, I thought you said your DUI occurred on April 26. The newspaper dated it as April 24. I don't get it."

Paul said, "Get the fuck out of my face." He left the house in anger.

Max and I were afraid Paul had a gun hidden somewhere in our new apartment.

We found a .38 caliber handgun in his dresser drawer. Max hid it in one of his gym shoes in his bedroom. Later we put the gun back, afraid of Paul's reaction if he found it missing.

On the following day Paul was fine. He acted as though all was well. He behaved like he had when we were younger and it fed my wish for life to be like this all the time. It was very seductive to have my husband back to being friendly and "normal."

A few weeks later on a beautiful day in May, Paul asked me to accompany him to our favorite lake. I was very excited and looked forward to the day together. But he disappeared that morning and never returned until late in the afternoon.

"I found a lot for our retirement home today. It's a knockout and I can't wait for you to see it," he said.

I was afraid to cast a cloud on this good bit of news, so I didn't ask why we didn't go to the lake. He obviously got a tip on a great lot and didn't want to miss out. I got in the car for a trip to see it. He drove a few miles west of town to a lovely new housing development with large homes on wooded lots. We got out of the car and he showed me the lot he had purchased for us. It was on a high hill filled with towering sturdy oaks. It was one of the most beautiful lots I had ever seen, with incredible views from all sides. We held hands and talked about the house plans.

He then drove me to another lot he had purchased in an adjacent development. The day was so filled with Paul's promises of a bright future I allowed myself to be seduced into believing it.

I didn't have a clue about how Paul was financing these purchases. He would tell me about real estate closings and I trusted that he would soon be filling our coffers. He had put down minimal amounts of earnest money to hold the lots he wanted. He was so confident about his down payments, I deluded myself that he had somehow regained control of our finances. It was good to see him positive and optimistic again.

My enthusiasm for the new plan was short-lived. A couple days later, Ann and I decided to go to a discount shopping mall across the state line. We'd both been hearing how popular it was and wanted to see it for ourselves. At one of the kitchen accessory shops, I hesitated about buying a small utensil. Later, in a clothing shop, I hesitated buying a purse I liked. Ann lost patience with me.

"Mom, why don't you wake up?" she asked. "Dad is spending your money left and right. He has put earnest money down on several lots you don't even know about. He told me not to tell you, so you wouldn't be mad at him. Wake up, Mom, or you won't have anything left. You hesitate to buy the smallest items and yet he is spending your money with abandon. I can't stand to watch while he does this to you."

I yelled back at her. "Ann, your father wouldn't betray me like that. You don't know him like I do."

"I know him better in some ways. Don't continue to put your trust in him."

I remember driving, crying and screaming at the same time. I should have pulled over. I couldn't believe or accept what Ann was telling me. But I loved her and also knew at some level she was telling me the truth. It was too ugly to believe, but I knew I'd better believe or it would be too late. Maybe it already was. We finished our trip in stony silence.

CHAPTER 22

I Want Out

On May 12, 1994, Paul asked, "Did you answer the phone this week and speak with Dennis, my real estate office manager?"

I was surprised Dennis had told Paul of his call to me. Dennis had called to tell me about finding Paul passed out at his desk in the wee hours of the morning two days before. He said there were bottles of alcohol strewn around his desk and more hidden in the drawers. Dennis claimed he had brought Paul home and dropped him off at our apartment and had settled him down on the living room sofa. I hadn't heard anything.

It was no longer unusual to have Paul gone for the night and absent in the morning. I had heard a lot of excuses and had stopped even trying to keep track of them. Dennis was surprised I didn't already know of the incident. I thanked him for the information, feeling it make a solid dent into my rusty armor of denial.

I asked him if he would be willing to work with me in arranging for an "intervention" with Paul. I would check with a treatment facility and make arrangements. I asked him to keep this quiet until I finalized things. He agreed.

Now I had no choice. I answered Paul. "Yes," I said. "I did speak briefly with Dennis two days ago."

"Do you mean to tell me that you didn't hang up on him immediately?" he continued.

"No I didn't," I said. "I thought you were on good terms with him, so why would I have hung up on him?"

"Because you're a damn fool and have betrayed me. You'll both pay for this."

"How did I betray you?" I asked. "And how will Dennis have to pay?"

"Shut up. You're a fool if you think I ever want to build a house with you." He went to the bedroom and grabbed the house plans he had been working on over the past year, crumbled them in a ball and shoved them in the wastebasket under the kitchen sink.

"I want a divorce!" he shouted.

I felt my breathing stop as though someone had belted me in the stomach.

"I can't believe you could throw away our twenty-five year marriage so easily. And solely because I answered the phone and spoke with Dennis?"

"I want out!" he bellowed. His face was red. Veins pulsed in his head where I'd never seen veins pulse before. He had dragon eyes, glazed and red. He looked both drunk and angry.

I stood up to him, scared and angry at the same time.

"I miss being your partner, Paul. I'm no longer included in any discussions when you make large purchases with our money. It's wrong for you to share with Ann and make her promise not to tell me. I'm your wife, not her."

"Well, I guess I can't trust her either, so I never want to see her again in my life. And I'm writing our minister and telling him I never want to see him again either. Now leave this apartment. Get out." he commanded.

"No, I have every right to live here." I stood very still, my legs planted. I wanted my feet to take root and not budge.

He walked toward me. I sensed I was about to be hit. I put my hands in front of my chest, palms out, to block any blows to my body. Paul pushed his body into me, but my hands helped deflect his advances.

He yelled, "Don't you ever touch me again!" He wrote something on our calendar and raced out of the apartment. I released a huge sigh. I read what he wrote: "Carol hit me."

Max came from his bedroom after Paul left. The color had drained from his face. He ran outside into the parking lot looking for his father. Through the window I could see Paul trying to hug Max, but Max refused and came back inside.

"Mom, are you OK? Dad has really flipped out. I don't know what he's going to do next."

"I know, honey, neither do I. I'm not sure where he is going, but I don't have a good feeling about it. You probably heard him ask me for a divorce. I wanted to do an intervention with him, but I think we've run out of time. I don't think we can pull it off. I'll try, though. As soon as I've taken my exam tomorrow, I'll go to the behavioral health unit of our hospital. I'll see if they can help me. I don't want you to worry. None of this is your fault. I'll take care of you, no matter what the outcome."

It was difficult after that scene to think about my licensure exam the next day. Paul knew I had been studying for it for the past six months and that my exam was tomorrow. I thought about the timing of his request for a divorce. Although he had been absent from home quite a bit, his anger must have been building for a long time. This incident was the last straw. Until then I hadn't realized he may have wanted me to fail the exam. He was really sick and I needed to help him.

CHAPTER 23

The Exam and a Note

My exam was ominously set for Friday the 13th. I wore a smiling mask for those I knew. They could not even guess the experience I'd had the night before. The exam itself was challenging, as I had suspected. The questions on family violence jumped out at me as if they'd been written just for me.

After the exam, I went to lunch with my two friends, but wasn't hungry. I had confided some tidbits of information to them, but I was vague about the details. They expressed concern and were supportive as usual. Next, I stopped at the local hospital's behavioral health center on my way home. I had been there so often for workshops on addictions. I had learned so much in that building from physicians and certified addictions counselors with years of experience. And now I was coming to arrange an intervention for Paul. I waited nervously in the waiting room, hoping none of my professional colleagues saw me to ask what I was doing. I could always tell them I was here on behalf of a client. They'd never question me.

The woman I met with about the intervention plan was savvy and direct. She had done interventions for years and took a very assertive stance. She would help me, but I would need to do my homework. I'd anticipated what was to come. I needed to find the most influential people in Paul's life to join me in the intervention. It may take a few weeks to gather folks and practice, so that the final confrontation would be done in a compassionate but powerful way. I liked the woman and thought I would be able to work with her.

As I drove home, I passed the real estate office and felt relief when I saw no yellow crime-scene tape. Paul hadn't made a specific threat, only a vague and negative reference to his office manager. But he was so angry at everyone, I was fearful. I wasn't sure what he was capable of at this point. When I got home I found the .38 was missing. What did that mean? What was his current thinking and feeling? His anger was more than targeted at me. It was more cosmic, directed at his universe. If I passed the exam, it would be a miracle. If I lived through this, it would be a bigger miracle.

I awoke the next morning; it felt too quiet for a Saturday. Paul must still be gone. Thank God. Max was still in bed. I started to brew some coffee when I noticed a big note on the refrigerator under a magnet. Paul's agenda for the day was written in bold, black marker. The note was filled with Paul's shorthand. I understood some of the realtor lingo. It said:

6:30 brkfst with B.J. and friends

7:00 -8:30 office call 4 customers

8:30-9:30??? Present offer on 196A listed @$15,000/A x .o25% commission.

Close 1ˢᵗ take out in Sept. / Oct. '94 $83.000 T. commission

9:30-12:00 home buyer $120-140,000, $3900 commission

1-6 or 7:00 Trip to JD County with Bank President

On 80A x $1600/A x .025%=$3200 commission

Possible $90,000 day. If I plan it OK.

This note, despite his passionate request for a divorce Thursday night, was extremely bizarre. His unfounded optimism was a very manic symptom. He was definitely cycling back into a euphoric state. His note became more difficult to read toward the end, his handwriting becoming almost illegible.

That night I was awakened at 11:00 p.m. Paul called to tell me he would be staying overnight at the Carollton Inn in another county many miles away. He ended the call by saying, "Bye, hun." He made a kissing sound over the phone. Did he forget his request for a divorce? Did he have any recall of the hideous things he'd said to me? He didn't sound like he wanted out now. This was crazy-making behavior. I almost imagined things were as they once were before he had slipped into mental illness. It was based on a wish, not on substance. I knew the reality now. I didn't have the courage to act on it yet.

There were other issues to deal with. Life is so multidimensional. Rarely do crises come neatly packaged and one at a time. They seemed to collide and grow exponentially.

I was not welcome at Jason's college graduation. Ann and Jason were still angry with me, because Paul took Ann's Toyota Supra for himself, even though he'd promised the car to her. She didn't direct her anger toward him, but toward me. I suspected she was angry at my prolonged marital loyalty. I understood. It was impossible to direct anger toward a mentally ill person. So useless. I found myself as frustrated as she was. No one could get angry at Paul anymore. It would be too dangerous. I felt helpless in making any changes. Mental illness and alcoholism were wrenching the life from our family. Leaving would probably be the best solution, but I wasn't ready yet.

The next weekend, I attended my school's annual retirement dinner for my friends alone. I actually enjoyed myself because I didn't have Paul to worry about in public with my friends. When I returned home later that evening, Paul watched me as I drove into the parking lot. He told me I looked pretty and complimented me on my "pretty pink suit." I thanked him but wondered about his remark; my suit was yellow. Perhaps it was the light in the parking lot. Perhaps he was under the influence. It might not have been a true statement, but at least it wasn't an angry one. It was a compliment, only bizarre. He drove away and I didn't even wonder where he was headed.

I walked inside our apartment and I thought about the school grant I still needed to write. I couldn't wait until the school year ended so I could focus on family issues. I fell asleep. Paul never made it to bed.

I hadn't been asleep long when the phone rang. It was my dad reminding me of my cousin's ordination celebration Mass the next day. I went alone. Paul hadn't come home last night and hadn't called to let me know what was going on. This would have alarmed me earlier in our marriage. Now I regarded it as normal.

I hadn't been in a Catholic Church for over twenty years. I sat with my dad and step-mother at Mass. I noticed the music had improved for Catholics since I was a little girl. How nice to see that the church allowed children to express joy. Church was somber and punitive when I was a child.

My aunt and uncle provided a nice dinner. They hadn't changed much over the years. I stayed after most of the guests had gone home, so I could tell my dad and stepmother about Paul and the intervention plan.

I took them aside out of the range of others' hearing.

"I don't know how to tell you this, but Paul has asked me for a divorce. He's been acting strange lately and I'm not sure what will happen, but want you to be prepared for the possible end of our marriage. I'm trying to arrange for an intervention, because I think Paul is depressed and is self-medicating with alcohol. So his problems are debilitating."

My dad said, "I thought Paul seemed different the last several times we got together, but I didn't realize he'd changed to that extent. Well, I don't know what else to say...."

My stepmom looked sad and said, "We've always liked Paul, but this doesn't sound like him. We'll be here for you, honey. Let us know what you need from us as it all plays out."

"Thank you," I said and gave them both a hug through my teary eyes.

They were great parents. I felt closer to my dad than I ever had and thanked God he'd found such a wise and loving woman to marry after my mom's death.

Although it seemed ironic that my cousin was getting ordained about the same time I was talking about getting a divorce, I was happy he was fulfilling an old dream of his. I thought back to the years when we had played "Mass" when we were children. He had always recruited me to be an altar boy.

As I returned to the plastic lawn chairs in my aunt's backyard, a cardinal sang to us from the top of a pine tree. He followed me here, I laughed to myself. I drove home in silence, thinking about my life's strange turn of events. My thoughts turned to preparation for the next school day. How was I going to fit everything in at work and begin gathering people to practice for Paul's intervention? It could be an exercise of several weeks. I hoped I could find enough willing people to help me.

CHAPTER 24

Felony DUI

It was a Monday that started out as any other, but I will never forget the date. I was in my cramped office at school rearranging papers on my desk, tossed there by several administrative assistants who helped organize my days. It was Monday, May 23, 1994, at 8:34 a.m. when my phone rang. Max was calling me from his school fifteen miles away. How odd. He'd never called me at work before.

"Mom, there's a rumor going around school saying Dad perpetrated a drive-by shooting. I'm leaving for the police department to find out more."

Words stuck in my mouth.

No, no, no screamed in my head! *Please God*, I uttered in silent prayer. *Tell me this isn't true.* "Yes, Max, go. I'm sure it's an ugly rumor, honey, but go ahead and investigate."

I put down the phone, almost unable to breathe. Something died inside me. I tried to stay in control. After putting down the receiver, my secretary called and told me I had three students in the outer office waiting to see me.

"Please reschedule them, Joyce. I have to make a call and I may be leaving the building. I'll get back to you."

I tried sounding composed. I knew my voice sounded irregular. Never had I left my desk without some valid reason. I stared at my calendar. At least nothing critical was scheduled for the day. I didn't have any special meetings during or after school. I was grateful.

My mind raced backwards in time. Paul had agreed to help facilitate our relationship group at church on Wednesday night. It sounded ridiculous in light of this new information. Could it even be true? I'd had so many good years with him and we had such a long history together. I thought about Paul cooking sausage and pancakes on Saturday mornings. I thought about him carving faces from the grapefruit rinds, entertaining the kids. Each one was sheer artistry and the kids would beg for more. I thought about all those tender notes he wrote and tucked into their lunch bags in the morning, giving them courage to do their best at school during the day. Paul had placed beautiful mums on our church front steps for the opening night of my divorce support group. Later he told me I made him proud. Memories flooded my mind. Many of them were good.

Could this be the same man? The man I married and loved with all my heart? I didn't want anyone to know what I was investigating. I hoped this was only a rumor. But another part of me knew it was true. I met Max at the police station. I drove the forty-minute commute to our hometown in less than thirty minutes. I was so anxious to get to the truth and to help Max make sense out of an absurd story. Max had already been talking to a detective. When I saw his face, I knew the story was true.

The officer invited us into his office and gave us details of the night before. My years of false hope about our future died in those few minutes. I knew what I had to do. I had to put Max and me and our future safety at the top of my list of priorities. I could no longer pretend, because pretending could be fatal.

I called our new Pastor Don and asked him if he could meet Max and me for lunch at Baker's Square. I didn't feel like eating, but I wanted to talk to someone Max and I both trusted. He was shocked by the day's news, but wasn't surprised when I told him I would be filing for divorce right after lunch. I expected him to tell me to go slowly. But twenty-six years had been time enough.

ACT

3

CHAPTER 25

My Family Law Attorney

I sat in the waiting room of an attorney one of my social worker friends had recommended. The thin veneer covering my sham of a marriage had finally been stripped away. I was filing for divorce. I had no more doubts. It had taken me twenty-six years to give up all hope of it getting better. I could no longer go on pretending. I thought about my own clients and the need for magazines in my waiting room. I tried thinking about anything but the reason I was sitting here. I made small talk with the paralegal behind the counter.

She said, "Bob is a great family attorney. He helped me with my own divorce two years ago. Trust me, two years from now you'll be laughing about today. I'm so much better off without my ex. I'm back in school, working part time, and I have plans to finish law school. Who knows? Someday I may be a full partner. I love the legal field. You've chosen the right lawyer."

"Well, I'm somewhat comforted. I never thought I'd be here myself. You see, I'd always helped others with their divorce issues. I lead divorce support groups and have counseled lots of troubled couples with both pre- and post-divorce issues. I guess there's no reason to think I'd have immunity just because I'm a marriage and family therapist."

"No, but I'm sure your background will help you through this. Bob should be out in a minute," she said. I was surprised by her casual tone and her use of his first name. Maybe this was intentional to help me feel more at ease. I'm sure I looked tense.

I couldn't concentrate on magazines. I used them as a prop. I kept ruminating about events leading up to this day, thinking if I pieced them together the right way, they would begin to make sense.

The paralegal returned and startled me.

"Bob will see you now," she said. I felt myself shudder a little.

I entered the regal attorney chambers. I took in lots of dark cherry wood and brown leather upholstery. Bob gestured for me to take a seat across from his acre- long desk. I summarized the day's events for him. He scanned a newspaper article on the corner of his desk and expressed shock, outrage and concern in equal measure.

"We'll take immediate action protecting you and your son, seeing how we can't predict when he'll be released at this point. I suggest a plenary or two- year order of protection for you, your married daughter and your son."

I was only mildly reassured since I had seen from experience how orders of protection were continually violated. I explained that Paul needed help, but I needed to file for divorce. The vestigial Catholic in me was somewhat surprised to hear myself say this. In the past, I overlooked Paul's refusal to get help. I was done with that. This was a new day in my life. Part of me was sad; part of me was scared. But a big part of me looked ahead to a future life without fear and disrespect.

At day's end on Monday, I picked up the newspaper and read the details about Paul's felony arrest in the early hours of the previous morning. It had been a very long day of piecing together what had happened. It was strange to now read about the events leading up to this moment.

The local papers claimed that at 2:20 a.m., Paul was charged with a felony DUI, aggravated fleeing and eluding, driving in the wrong lane, aggravated assault, battery and unlawful use of weapons. His driver's license was suspended for two years. He allegedly pointed a .38 handgun at a man I'd never heard of before. According to the news release, he grabbed the man and pulled his shirt off his chest. Twelve witnesses said Paul had been drinking heavily at a restaurant west of town before his arrest. He was carrying a concealed weapon at the time. Multiple news articles claimed he had pistol- whipped a man in the parking lot. He had also visited an auto body shop on the outskirts of town and shot out several car and truck windows, as well as windows in the shop itself. It was owned by someone Paul had real estate dealings with. The name of the shop owner was familiar to me, but I had never met him. I didn't understand why he had selected this man's business. He had talked about him negatively a few times, but I hadn't understood the magnitude of his anger toward him. Later, I was allowed to read the police reports and they supported the stories I had read in the newspapers.

With Paul in jail and refusing to speak with anyone, including me, I was left to think more about the events leading up to his felony DUI. For many years, I felt that Paul and I had functioned reasonably well without alcohol. Neighbors had teased us with labels like "Mr. and Mrs. Diet Coke." But there had been many moments interspersed with the good times that were beyond my ability to explain. It seemed as if we had both busied ourselves with work and kids and distracted ourselves from reality.

I had been waging my own psychological war for so many years. I knew things were not all right with Paul or with our relationship. I wondered about Paul's resolve not to drink. I wondered about vodka. I knew I had to study alcoholism more. I read about myself in books on co-dependency and enabling. I decided at that moment to become a certified alcohol and drug counselor. It helped me understand the cunningness of the disease and the denial others faced with alcoholism in their families. I had been a family therapist for many years. So, how could this happen? How could I be so empowered by my education and professional experience and yet be so victimized by mental illness and alcoholism in my own marriage? I felt overwhelming shame and guilt.

CHAPTER 26

The Healing Power of Friendship

Paul had put money down on several rural lots in a new development west of town. He warned Ann not to tell me. Ann told me he didn't think I'd approve of what he'd done. And now here I was, pursuing a divorce with even more chaos. Even my "Protestant side" was somewhat surprised, but I stifled that and focused on our safety and coming to terms with my new reality. I left my attorney's office two hours after my first visit armed with multiple forms that I barely understood. I knew I was embarking on a formidable journey that would change my life, but at this point, I couldn't know the details of how.

I drove home to meet Max and let him know what I'd done at the attorney's office. I drove by the sign at our second temporary home in two years: the apartment at Firethorn. What a prophetic name. Had Paul ever intended to build our maintenance-free home? I had been holding onto a false promise and fantasy for too long.

I walked into our kitchen and my eyes landed on the red light flickering on the answering machine. It had recorded forty-seven messages. Some of the messages were from Paul's former students expressing shock and disbelief at the newspaper article and radio announcements about his arrest. Some of them said Paul was the best instructor they'd ever had. Some were from friends in our former neighborhood where we'd lived for twelve years. They couldn't believe the rumors, but they had heard everything on the radio or they'd read the paper. They didn't know what to think. Maybe, some suggested, this was a case of mistaken identity. One man's voice sounded sinister. He didn't identify himself. He said Paul should call him at a certain number if he wanted to go through with a purchase. How mysterious. It didn't sound like a real estate call.

For the last three months, on the nights Paul stayed home, he had been getting up at about 4:00 a.m. to go to the gas station three blocks away. He said he had friends to see there. I knew this was strange, but I'd learned to accept this as normal behavior. I had stretched the range of normal way too far, but so gradually I hardly even noticed.

Paul often got by on two hours of sleep a night. This had become normal, too. Sometimes when Paul had been hammering or sawing in the garage at 2:00 a.m., the kids would ask me if I could "make Daddy stop." My requests had fallen on deaf ears, much like my previous suggestions concerning professional help. I had imagined filing for divorce back then. How would I have answered the question of "why?" I would have had to say because he behaves strangely, for example, hammering and sawing through the night. He may have bipolar disorder, but refuses to get evaluated by a psychiatrist.

I remember reading *Codependent No More* and hating it. I didn't like looking at myself in that much depth. It was far easier to use my new insights to help others who were struggling with similar issues rather than work on my own. I forced myself to reread it. Some paragraphs I reread several times. I knew this book was written for me, but I also fought the concepts laid out so clearly. I expertly deflected and depersonalized it for myself, reviewing cases I was currently working on to see how I could apply this book to couples and families I had in my private practice.

Each time I brought up to Paul the need to get a professional assessment, I was told, "I don't need a damned shrink like you telling me what's good for me."

"I'm not asking you to see someone like me, Paul. I'd like you to see a doctor to help you sleep through the night."

This grandiose Paul, this Paul who appeared to be suffering from bipolar disorder, wasn't the Paul I knew, loved and married. At least, I had told myself, he appeared to be maintaining sobriety. Now that assumption was even in question. According to the police reports, he wasn't doing that, either.

The next morning began with a phone call. My friend Sharon invited me to breakfast at the neighborhood park down by the river. "I read the newspaper," she said. "I'll pick you up around 9:00 a.m. with some coffee, juice and warm muffins." I immediately accepted her invitation; it sounded so normal and I needed normal right now.

Sharon pulled up in her silver mini-van. I could smell the fresh-baked muffins. I was grateful to have a close friend I could trust. She drove to Palisade Park on the Green River. We carried our breakfast to the picnic table nearest the river's edge. As we unpacked our breakfast, Sharon said, "I've read the paper and heard the newscasts on the radio. You don't have to talk about anything at all, but I'll listen if you want."

Her approach was masterful with the exact right tone. I did need to talk with someone I trusted, and there was no one I preferred more than Sharon to confide in. I gave her the latest update. She had also been raised Catholic and could appreciate my reluctance to file for divorce. But she didn't judge and could understand my pursuit of it after all that had happened with Paul.

I told her things I hadn't told anyone. "I had bought a new toothbrush and one night it was missing. When I asked Paul, he claimed he hadn't seen it. So, I bought another one. Several days passed and one morning I needed to use a lint remover. As I rummaged through Paul's handkerchief drawer, I found a small handgun facing my missing toothbrush. I jumped a little when I saw them together.

"That was weird, Carol," Sharon said.

"Paul would say I overreacted to his behavior."

"No, that was weird."

"Paul is often gone during the night. I roll over in bed and he's gone. One night I woke to the smell of sausage cooking, and it was 2:00 a.m. I went into the kitchen and Paul was standing over the stove, cooking sausage."

"Carol, I needn't tell you that's not normal behavior. It's crazy behavior."

"You're right. The following night around the same time, I heard the washing machine agitating. I went to look and I found Paul standing in the laundry room. He said he had noticed that Max's socks were starting to look gray so he thought he would bleach and wash them. Later that week, he was in the driveway changing the oil in our car at 4:00 a.m. When I asked why, he'd say the job needed to be done. No doubt his behavior is bizarre, but no one will lock him up for it. Nor is he willing to get help for it.

"Sharon, I read the police report about his alleged assault with a deadly weapon at a local bar. The police interviewed twelve witnesses who said Paul held a gun to a man's head in the parking lot. Paul claimed it was the sprayer nozzle for a garden hose. Then Paul shot up an auto body shop and several vehicles parked outside. I think he's delusional and totally out of touch with reality."

"I'd have to agree. He sounds damned crazy to me," Sharon said.

"We didn't have the $20,000 to make a farm payment last year, so we had to sell the farm. I was so relieved after we sold that place. We didn't make anything, but I'm glad we got out from under it.

In the meantime, I'd been working hard and saving as much as I could for both of the kids and their college funds. But as fast as I tried to save it, it disappeared. Against my advice, he bought another home, a rental property. We've sold our own home now, but we have a rental property. We didn't have the money for these wild investments, but he wouldn't take my advice on anything. If I don't get some legal and financial protection, Paul will go through all of our money and there won't be anything left for either of the kids.

"Ann told me Paul confided in her about putting earnest money down on several lots. He feared my disapproval because he thinks I'm not enough of a risk-taker. This divide-and-conquer strategy is so common with alcoholics. They confide different things to different people, but no one gets the full, true story. Maybe his arrest helped me realize this couldn't continue forever and I'd have to get a divorce if I were ever to get any control of my life. His manic episodes are terrifying, Sharon."

She sipped her coffee. "I think you are doing the right thing, Carol. You must protect both your physical and financial self. Ann is married now, but you do have to consider Max, and try to give him a future. You want him physically safe and you do want something left in your savings to help him with college."

"You're right, Sharon. I'm afraid Paul's already spent so much money that we'll never recover. I need to stop the bleeding now, or Max won't have anything left for college. This divorce won't be inexpensive, either. I don't expect it to be contested, but my attorney says the divorce may cost me more with Paul in jail. Why, I'm not sure."

"Carol, I've known Paul for years. Our whole family has. This all sounds so unlike him. Has he been drinking at all throughout this?"

"You know, he'd been doing very well avoiding alcohol for the past eleven years, or so I thought. I wondered about him on April Fools' Day this year. It was Good Friday. Our family had always attended Good Friday church services for the past twenty-six years.

This year, Paul announced we would all be going to a B.B. King concert in Merrillville, Indiana. He told Max to invite a friend, which he did. I thought this was an unusual plan, but I wanted to avoid a big conflict, so I didn't say anything. I usually took the route of avoiding conflict whenever given a chance. I have been an over-the-top people-pleaser who is still in need of a recovery program. Anyway, at the concert Paul was so agitated he couldn't stay in his seat. He went out to the lobby about six times during the concert. On the way home, he was speeding and got a ticket from a female police officer. He got into a big debate with her and tried to deflect his offense to another driver who was traveling close to us. He was convinced the other guy ahead of us was going faster than the speed limit and the radar gun must have incorrectly targeted the wrong plates. Later he got the ticket dismissed from court. I'll never know how. I think he was speeding and I was shocked when he told me it had been thrown out of court."

"I guess I hadn't heard about that," Sharon added. "I'm surprised you didn't file for divorce long ago."

"I've thought about that a lot. When I feel guilty about it now, I ask myself why it took me this long. Perhaps I should have filed earlier. I've come up with a few theories. Perhaps it was connected to some invisible loyalty to my mom. She had a very troubled marriage with my dad, but never divorced. She hung in there, because he would never consider divorce and she had no where to go. She'd been a stay-at-home mom and wouldn't have known how to survive. During the '60s the social climate would have been more disapproving of her than me. I'd read a book once called *Invisible Loyalties* and I may have had some of those unconscious motives playing out in my life.

"Another reason I chose to stay," I continued, "is the seductive nature of normalcy. Because his episodes were sporadic and often spaced very far apart, Paul was capable of returning to his prior stable self. I allowed myself to think I'd been making too big of a deal out of bizarre events and behaviors. I loved the comforting routine of predictability. He was such an extraordinary husband

and dad when our customary routine kicked in. He was often a full partner with me and great father for the kids. He enjoyed cooking, redecorating, collecting and refinishing antiques, having friends over, parent-teacher conferences. I'm still baffled about how intermittent this disease is, much like alcoholism, but a dual enemy. My third reason to stay was overwhelming *fear*. I had married immediately out of college and had gone from my parents' home to my husband without ever having lived independently. I felt woefully inadequate to survive on my own. Add to that my responsibility for Max, with massive amounts of debt."

Sharon listened to my sordid tale without judgment. She didn't prescribe solutions or deride me. She simply listened with an understanding and compassion that made it all right to think all of this through. And so I continued.

"On the following Sunday after the B.B. King incident, I invited my parents to join us for Easter dinner. In the past, I always baked a ham. This year I decided to make Paul's favorite dish, lasagna. I made the same recipe I've always made and after dinner, he stood up and announced, 'This lasagna tastes like shit. I don't want you to ever cook an Italian dinner again.' Then he left.

"I thought about anhedonia. Cocaine addicts often lose pleasure in everything but their use of cocaine. Paul no longer took pleasure in his favorite dishes. I thought of several explanations for his behavior. We all sat there looking at each other with blank stares, as though we had each been hit in the face. The words stung more than a physical hit."

"Well, I told him I wouldn't make the dish again, and here I'd thought it was a family favorite. Everyone else said it was delicious. After Paul ran outside in his disgust over dinner, my dad said there was something wrong with Paul. I agreed with him saying I wished I could have him hospitalized for verbal abuse, lack of gratitude and general unpleasantness."

"Less than a month after this dinner, he was arrested for a DUI in an adjacent county. He went to jail and then to Good Samaritan Hospital. The odd thing was I didn't see him and he didn't tell me until two days later. But he told me he had been arrested on April 26, not the 24. So on April 27, I bought a newspaper reporting his arrest date as April 24. (Later on I found both a police report and an ambulance bill citing April 24.) When I asked Paul about the discrepancy, he said, 'Get the f— out of my face.' "

"There is never a good or convenient time to file for divorce, Sharon, but this latest incident couldn't have come at a worse time. Max is getting ready to take his ACT exam. We should be checking out colleges right now. I'm still trying to keep up with my full-time high school position and my private practice two nights a week."

"Work helps distract me. I feel most at peace when I am helping others. I don't want to start taking antidepressants. I have so many friends using them, but I refuse. But I have to start facing the reality of the collapse of my marriage."

"You didn't want to or couldn't see it before. But now it's time to put your safety and Max's first," said Sharon.

It was good to talk to Sharon. She helped me by being a good listener and being honest with me. I had never needed a good friend more in my entire life. And she was with me. She listened and it felt great to be heard.

CHAPTER 27

Surviving Financially

My parents came to celebrate Memorial Day. They took Max and me to lunch at our favorite Norwegian restaurant. It was a nice break. My days had been spent on the phone returning endless phone calls: to the CPA, attorney or his paralegal; people answering my ads about things for sale, and supportive friends offering words of comfort. I felt grateful for family and friends. I prayed school would be over soon. I was having trouble focusing on the grant I should have been writing.

I found myself in a more serious financial situation than I had previously thought. I visited our bank to check on available funds and discovered our joint bank account had been reduced to about two hundred dollars. The last time I had looked, a few days before, there had been close to $13,000.in our checking account. Paul had withdrawn most of the money a few days before he went to jail. In addition, I had opted for my school salary to be dispensed on a nine-month rather than a twelve- month cycle. In the past, I hadn't needed extra money in the summer, since Paul worked throughout the year. I soon realized the bad timing involved with this decision. I might have a few private practice clients over the summer, but many of those clients would disappear due to vacations and new schedules.

This was also the season we should have been exploring college choices with Max. Now, however, I just wanted to survive. I kept trying to erase the picture of a homeless bag lady with a son from my visual imagery.

Our lease was close to expiring on the apartment at Firethorn. I had wanted to buy a small townhouse for Max and me, but now I didn't have money for a down payment. I knew the banks wouldn't approve a loan with borrowed money for a down payment, but I wondered if my father might be willing to help. I couldn't believe that at the age of forty-eight, I was in this humble position. I was so angry at mental illness.

My father and stepmom were shocked by the news. They had always liked Paul and he'd been like a second son to my dad. I was thinking about selling possessions in order to survive the summer. I would do whatever I could to keep Max living in a decent neighborhood and to protect his college future.

I had been making over one hundred thousand dollars a year, but my earnings were all in the joint account with Paul. I discovered he was hiding a ten- thousand -dollar credit card debt. Our car insurance agent had checked out the impounded Toyota Supra and said my policy was being cancelled because they were concerned Paul could somehow have access to my car. I explained to my agent I was filing for divorce, but that wasn't enough reassurance for him. Luckily a competing firm was happy to enroll me.

Paul's Toyota Supra was still under lock and key. Our Toyota Cressida was missing. Our older Toyota truck was missing as well. I eventually found it near a Baskin-Robbins ice cream shop.

I was terrified to testify about Paul and his bizarre behavior. All my previous encounters in front of a judge had been professional, but this would be different. I was dreading it. Could this experience enable me to have greater empathy for the people I worked with? I told myself it could be the good coming out of a bad situation.

I thought about my immediate need for cash and all of the used equipment sitting on one of our remaining farms. The tractors and plows were rusting in the fields. I decided to advertise the used equipment to some local farmers. Within a week I had an offer on an old tractor for fifteen hundred dollars. The offer seemed fair and I arranged to sell the tractor over the phone. The check arrived. We would stretch this money over the summer until my paychecks started to come again in the fall.

I started eyeing my antiques in a different way. Now they were pieces that could be exchanged for food. I would exhibit them at an outdoor antique show. I rented a booth and planned to sell what I could. Max and I loaded dressers, tables, iron accessories, brass candlesticks and antique beds into the bed of our old Toyota truck. We made a little money and I felt we did well enough, even though I sold a cast- iron rabbit for thirty-five dollars while an identical one at the booth next door sold for three hundred and fifty. Was my desperation beginning to show? We both needed food more than antique, cast- iron rabbits.

I made my first appearance at court for the "discovery" process. In "discovery," the divorcing couple submits a list of assets and liabilities to their attorneys, so they and the judge can view each person's complete economic situation. I included the farm equipment and antiques I had sold. The judge told me I couldn't sell anything else without court permission. I was grateful I had sold things when I did, which enabled us to keep room and board for the summer. It appeared as though the remaining farms would be sold or foreclosed on, as well as the new rental property Paul had recently purchased. I didn't like the "foreclosure" idea and I vowed to fight this with all I had.

Our plenary, or two-year order of protection, was granted. It encompassed the children and me. Paul was given a copy. He sent me a letter from jail expressing his fury. He referred to my "phony fear" regarding him. One judge inquired about other guns on the property. I told him I wasn't sure, but it was possible Paul could have other guns hidden around. He told me to make a thorough search and bring any guns I found to the county jail for holding until further notice. I promised him I would.

Max and I went through the storage facility, which held all our extra furniture from our former home. We found eight guns. There were rifles and shotguns. We didn't find any other handguns. One was confiscated the night Paul was arrested. There could have been another, but I wouldn't know where else to look. Max also found a paper bag filled with miniature vodka bottles in a secret stash for self-medicating.

I made two trips to the jail after school that week to deliver Paul's guns. I rang the buzzer at the jail's entrance. I stated my name and told the deputy I had found more guns, which the judge ordered returned to jail. I was still dressed in my suit and heels carrying one gun at a time from my trunk. I was probably an odd -looking sight. I felt better having them safely tucked away. When Paul used them to go hunting, I thought nothing about them. Now, I was glad to be rid of them.

On June 12, 1994, Max left with our church youth group for a trip to Minnesota and the boundary waters. I was delighted he liked canoeing and being a member of a good youth group. He needed to be away from all the difficulties.

I was able to make the mortgage payment on the rental property and my private practice office that month. I was feeling grateful and relieved. I joined in the school's annual golf outing. Paul had his first court date, but it didn't pertain to me, so I barely thought about it.

CHAPTER 28

Stormy Lake

Several weeks later, my friend Marcy invited Max and me to visit her home on Stormy Lake near Eagle River, Wisconsin. We were happy to accept. Max, now eighteen, water-skied for the first time. He was a natural. He looked ready for a professional water-ski team, at least from his mom's perspective. It was great seeing him happy again. I tried water-skiing without much success. Perhaps being forty-eight and not eighteen had some bearing on it. Not being in good shape was also a major factor. I was able to get up on the kneeboard. Marcy called out, "Are you thinking about your divorce now?"

"No," I yelled back. "I'm trying to stay alive." What fun. Max and I loved driving her speedboat.

Later that summer, we helped Ann and Jason move from their college town to a new home about twenty miles away. They would both be closer to their workplaces and closer to us. I was so glad we were speaking again.

Max amazed me. He seemed more of a man at eighteen than a boy. His adulthood was foisted upon him very abruptly. He was able to get our lawn mower running and installed a new battery. He also put a new fuel filter in his truck when it broke down on the highway. He was taking responsibility very well and I felt blessed having such a great son.

At the end of the month, Max went to an engineering camp at the state college. I was thankful they admitted him, even though I was late with his registration fee. He was happy to attend with his best friend.

I'd been trying to track down our tax and real estate transactions, which was almost a full-time job. I just couldn't believe I'd given Paul my total trust for twenty-six years.

One day the dishwasher broke, flooding the kitchen. My bad credit rating arrived in the mail that afternoon. I felt as though I was sinking into an abyss. The bad news kept coming. In the midst of this, I saw my cardinal. His song was as beautiful as ever. Is God sending him my way in my lowest moments? Before my marital distress I'd never paid attention to a little thing like a cardinal, but now I noticed the simplest things. I'd never been so poor and also felt so close to God.

I asked our family physician, Dr. F., if he could get some medical attention for Paul's broken shoulder in the county jail. I had requested help from two judges, our state's attorney, my divorce attorney and two psychiatrists about the same thing. The consensus was that a complete medical and psychological evaluation would be in order. Unfortunately, Dr. F.'s contract with the county to provide medical evaluations for the prisoners had expired the previous year. There was no longer money in the county budget for any evaluations at the county jail.

CHAPTER 29

Burying the Old Dream

The lot Paul and I had once planned for our retirement home had been sold. It was one of the most beautiful home sites I'd ever seen. But the dream died several months ago and it was time to bury it for good. My attorney called and said Paul was about to be bonded out of jail, but had been badly beaten by another inmate prior to his release. I was feeling sad for him and his plight, but I was also concerned about his anger toward me since he was being released. Max and I needed to leave town for a few days.

We flew to Kansas City to visit Ann's in-laws over my birthday, the fourth of July. When Max and I arrived at their home, we sat out on their beautiful shady deck. We were both exhausted and fell asleep for three hours. Sleep without fear felt delicious to us.

Ann's mother-in-law took us all on a trolley car ride and high tea at the Ritz- Carlton. Kansas City was so beautiful, with its fountains and statuary in the plaza. We attended BBQ's Blues Fest in the evening and enjoyed musicians named Roma, Mama Rae and Zoe. I wanted to be around strong, funny and outrageous women. I laughed for the first time in months.

We attended a Royal's baseball game followed by fireworks on my forty-eighth birthday. We visited the Arabia Steamboat Museum the following day. The museum included a sunken steamboat from 1856 filled with two tons of cargo. I never would have expected to find a buried ship recovered from a Kansas cornfield. But then again, would I ever have expected to be divorcing after twenty-six years? It occurred to me how much of life is tentative. How often do our plans and expectations go awry? I had lost the life I once thought I knew. I was beginning to reclaim something new in its place, but wasn't quite sure what it would look like.

At the end of the week, Max and I took a late flight and arrived back home at 2:00 a.m. on Sunday, July 10.

Two weeks later, a once- important day arrived. July 20, 1994 would have been our twenty-sixth anniversary. Technically, it still was, since we were only in the process of divorce. Nothing was final yet in a legal sense. In my heart and soul it was over. There was no joy left for my marriage; only sadness, anger and regret. That day, I vowed to start treating July 20 as any other day.

I had been a family therapist in denial and a very codependent addictions counselor. I saw my children paying a high price for my doomed vision. I had always wanted the best for them. I wished I had recognized Paul's early symptoms of mental illness in the beginning stages. But I still didn't know when that was. Sleeplessness, sleep apnea, metabolic syndrome, ADHD, alcoholism, uncontrolled spending, grandiosity, paranoia and euphoria blurred together in visual images and tiny vignettes. It was such an array of symptoms, but I couldn't pin down a date. This intense retrospection needed to stop if I was to move forward.

My girlfriends who were going through their divorces kept suggesting antidepressants for me; since I wasn't sleeping well. I knew most of them were taking them, and I knew I could be at risk for depression, but I resisted and vowed to seek out as many healthy alternatives as possible. I joined an aerobic step class at our community recreation center. I felt very clumsy at first, but I loved how I felt after a good cardio workout. Ignoring the fact that most students in my class were about thirty years younger than me helped me survive. I began sleeping better right away.

I started reading Melodie Beattie's meditation book. I'd enjoyed her workshop in New Orleans once and always found her writing inspirational. I felt good about my new resolve to start walking with my girlfriends three times a week. My body craved movement. I was about twenty-five pounds overweight. I had been so busy working, I had neglected my body. How had I not noticed? I registered at Aerobics Plus for a week's free trial. I scheduled another weekend at Stormy Lake.

I recalled recent good memories. I had tried some things I had never tried before. I'd ridden on a kneeboard and driven a speedboat. I visited some friends in their summer home in Holland, Michigan. I splurged on a five- dollar dried flower bouquet at the local Farmer's Market. My friends and I visited Saugatuck as well. I remembered feeling joy-filled moments. It felt good to be valued and respected again. And it felt so good to laugh. I stayed in an all -white wicker room that overlooked Lake Michigan. I felt the tension I'd been holding melt away.

I didn't know where Paul was now or if he'd been released from jail. He hadn't been by the house to pick up his belongings while I was gone. He may have feared running into Max or me and violating the orders of protection. I learned the Toyota Supra, which he had purchased for Ann, was no longer impounded but sat in the local Toyota dealer's parking lot.

My attorney called to tell me the little post-a-notes and unopened letters in Paul's briefcase showed more than a few outstanding bills. One example he gave was the $6,000.00 overdue on our 1992 income taxes. Paul had always told me I worried too much and to leave everything pertaining to finances up to him.

I paid for Max's canoe trip. The church offered to pay Max's fees, but I declined the offer; I didn't want to accept charity. I was proud we had both survived this long summer.

CHAPTER 30

Making Room for New Dreams

I wanted Max to stay in the same hometown school district. Fall was soon approaching and I needed to find a home. I learned if I didn't buy another home by November 5, I would owe the IRS another $14,000 in capital gains. Paul had insisted on selling our home almost two years before, but now I was going to have to figure out a way to buy another home or go in debt even more. I wanted to buy a townhome to create new memories for Max and me, but I wasn't sure how to go about it without money.

My dad had offered to loan me the down payment. I was grateful to him for coming though for us in our most desperate time. My brother had also gone through a divorce in Sarasota, Florida. He considered heading north to find a job. I told him I would give him a place to live if I had a home by the time he visited. His wife had locked him out and decided to marry his best friend. He was hurting as much as I was. My poor Catholic father never expected to see his two children divorcing, and especially not at the same time.

By August 5, 1994 I had made an offer on a townhouse in a place called Maplewood. The sellers accepted it. I couldn't believe it. A brand new home. Now I had to get approval by a mortgage company. I discovered I needed more for a down payment than I was first told. Max's godfather was willing to loan me another $4000 to make it happen. I needed a bank to help me despite my divorce, debt and damaged credit. I was asking for a bloomin' miracle.

As soon as I returned to school that fall and started receiving a paycheck again, I could go about repaying people. I had to get beyond the news that Paul had not paid the $10,000 balance on our credit card for Ann's wedding. I was also not going to worry too much about the IRS and the back taxes I owed them since they had agreed to a $200 monthly installment plan. Paul wrote to tell me he had paid all of our taxes, but I couldn't let myself believe that. The IRS had a different version.

If I figured in the total cost of two lost homes, three farms, earnest money put down on property, credit card and tax debt, the sum total was about $500,000. This was not an easy sum to acknowledge from a coupon-clipping, generally thrifty wife and mother. It was almost laughable when I thought about the many times I had gone bargain-hunting to garage sales with my girlfriends and bought clothes on sale when I could. I spent hours gardening, canning and freezing food to save money. I sewed my children's clothing, crafted homemade Christmas gifts and candles for family and friends. I questioned the relative value of anything I had done. Nothing seemed to make sense anymore.

On August 21, 1994, two very special things occurred. First, it was Ann's 22nd birthday. She was so beautiful and such a wonderful daughter. We'd had our struggles, but I'd never stopped loving her. Even in our darkest moments, I have loved her and have always had enormous pride in her.

Second, Max and I learned we would have a new home. I had been approved for a loan on the townhouse. My former boss offered us boxes and muscles for help on moving day. What a welcome relief, since I had no moving funds set aside. One of his sons worked for Mayflower and so his expert help would be very welcome.

No one knew where Paul was. Or if anyone did know, no one told Max or me.

On Saturday, September 3, we moved across town. Max and I were exhausted by day's end, but delighted to be in our new home with no bad memories. Ann helped us a lot. We were close to Max's high school and my workplace. It was so good to be in a new home. Thank you, God.

It didn't take long for Max and me to get into a comfortable routine. We hadn't spoken to Paul since he had gone to jail. And with the orders of protection, it was possible we would meet in court for our final dissolution of marriage.

I had heard rumors he was possibly living with his sister in the country back in our hometown. We'd been friends for thirty-two years, but most of Paul's relatives had stopped speaking to Max and me. They couldn't understand what had happened to him, or what could warrant his going to jail. He had always been the most successful one in the family. It must have been very difficult for them to comprehend everything that had happened. It was hard for his immediate family, so how can one explain it to others? They didn't want to hear my explanation at the time.

I had felt God's presence with us with every step. Somehow, after losing everything, I'd never felt closer to Him. Maybe this is what I needed to learn for courage to grow. Lose the "stuff" and find my path through faith in Him.

CHAPTER 31

The Continuing Burden of my Years of Denial

The financial problems continued throughout the summer and fall of 1994. My two immediate worries at the end of summer were the $33.00 in my checking account and the tenants in the rental property Paul had leased out. They had been falling further behind in their rent. Their $6000 in back rent would go a long way in an empty savings account. I thought if they could pay a little toward that end, I would be happy. After checking the lease agreement Paul had written for them, I noticed he had scratched out any conditions that would have established some important boundaries in a lease agreement.

Waiting for the rent check to arrive after countless phone calls and letters was not proving successful. Three letters to Curtis and Sonia, our renters, had netted zero response. I had no choice but to go to the house and request the back rent in person.

I had not purchased this home, but it was done with my money and against my wishes. Paul hadn't needed my signature to purchase this home, but now I needed to deal with Paul's decision and my blindness. I drove across town one night after supper and rang the doorbell. Curtis came to the door and I introduced myself as their landlady who had been sending them letters about past-due rent. Curtis invited me in. I sat down on the living room sofa. I had never been in the house before and I was curious about what I co-owned with Paul. The first thing I noticed was six children under the age of five and a very pregnant Sonia. The second thing I noticed was the abysmal, physical state of the home itself. It smelled of baby vomit and dogs and cats. The pets were so numerous, I lost count after several attempts. I couldn't count them all but I could smell them. Stains covered the threadbare carpeting and magic markers decorated the walls.

Curtis explained he and Sonia wanted to pay their back rent, but they were still catching up on medical bills; he had been laid off awhile back. He said his mom had been helping with some of the bills, but couldn't continue to bail them out. He mentioned she worked as a counselor in a drug treatment center, and as I connected the dots, I realized his mom would have been the one doing Paul's intervention if we'd had enough time. Curtis took a long drag on a cigarette and continued, "The way I see it, Carol, I could bust my ass and try to find work or I could sit on my ass and let unemployment checks roll in."

It was obvious to me which path Curtis had chosen. I decided to appeal to his sense of logic.

"The difficulty I see with your plan not to pay your rent, Curtis, is the very real threat I face of foreclosure. My mortgage company would like the monthly payment and since my soon-to-be ex-husband is now unemployed, (I eliminated any reference to jail) I can't make those payments without your help. So, we have about six months until you have no home to rent and I won't be your landlady." Not only did this news fail to alarm Curtis in the way I presumed it might, he appeared totally unfazed by the news.

I continued to observe the little ones drawing on the walls with crayons as the dogs defecated on the carpet. Pregnant Sonia kept chain smoking and looked as though she might deliver a child or two any moment.

Curtis offered me a check for $300.00 and I accepted it, but left knowing I would talk to my attorney and start an eviction process. Max and I would need to work together preparing the home for sale to avoid foreclosure. Until the eviction process began, I made monthly trips to the house to see if Curtis might write me another check toward his rent. It was a waste of time.

My attorney agreed to help me in the eviction process, but it would take some time. The sooner we started the better. We needed to give the family sufficient warning so they could find alternate housing. I felt very bad about this. I had never had to evict anyone before, especially a family with young children and a pregnant mother. I also knew Max and I couldn't live rent free anywhere, so I would need to pursue this if we were going to survive.

I updated Pastor Don when he asked how things were going for us. He offered to get a team of volunteers together when we had completed the eviction. He said they could help us clean, paint and repair broken windows. What a wonderful offer. I had not expected anything this good. I swallowed my pride and accepted the offer. I knew there was no way I could possibly afford to restore this house without help. If I let the foreclosure proceed it could further erode my ability to help Max with college. I told him I would let him know when the eviction was completed and we could start work.

CHAPTER 32

Was it Love or Was it Vodka?

In August of 1994, some of my divorced friends invited me to visit the Oasis Center downtown. It was a social event with other single and divorced people. I was still legally married. I was not dating and had no desire for it, but I was previewing my new life as a single person. There were many unchartered waters out there. I felt too old for this.

The Oasis Center was supposed to be a therapeutic setting for singles led by professional facilitators. Neal was our facilitator and he reminded me of Stuart Smalley from Saturday Night Live. A feeling of desperation hung in the air, even though everyone sat on big fluffy pillows and tried to assume a relaxed posture. Men and women were in equal numbers in a very large living room. One man said he'd never married and was now regretting he hadn't. Another guy claimed he wanted marriage because he was a "slob" and couldn't afford a housekeeper. A third gentleman explained he needed a woman who didn't mind him sleeping a lot and who liked caring for numerous cats.

My friend Diane had driven and we returned home at 2:30 a.m. Her car had sputtered and died for lack of gas as we entered her driveway. I was grateful it hadn't died on the expressway. It seemed a fitting end to the night's event.

Thanksgiving Day fell on November 24 in 1994. I received a phone call from Paul in the evening. He had vanished for months and now he called me crying. I could tell he'd been drinking. He was living in a trailer somewhere out in the country.

"I love you, Carol, and I will always love you," he said. I was astonished and speechless. But the sound which came from my mouth was a mystery to me. It was something between a laugh and a cry.

I think it was a bit of a shriek. "Oh, Paul, why did all this happen?" I knew how pathetic my question sounded, but I was in shock. It was the first time he had called me after months of silence. He said, "I don't know what to say," and then he hung up.

My term as president of one of the state divisions for my professional organization began in this same month. For the past year, I had served as president-elect. I had wanted to keep Paul's situation quiet, but that wasn't possible with a media hungry for stories. This would be remembered as a year of feeling both shamed and honored at the same time.

I was looking forward to the National Conference in November at a very prestigious hotel in a nearby city. I was invited to introduce Maurizio Andolphi and Salvadore Minuchin. It was a culmination of a dream for me. I had always admired these pioneers in the field of family therapy. I loved the anticipation prior to the conference.

As much as I looked forward to the conference, I dreaded going to my mailbox each day after I arrived home from school. I dreaded it for two reasons: my neighbors and my bills. My townhouse complex had a communal mailbox with thirty-two small locked cubicles. It served as a public gathering place where familiar strangers chatted about the weather or complained about how late the mail was. It was the only time and place I saw any neighbors. Almost everyone offered a polite smile and courtesy greeting. I found this hard to do. I felt like crying. I knew these were ordinary citizens. Did they know my story? I feared the reactions of these virtual strangers. I hated my mailbox more because it was so often filled with bad news or bills from my attorney's office or the IRS.

One day I mentioned my distaste of going to my mailbox to my friend, another therapist named Sylvia. I told her I'd tried to vary the time I went, sometimes waiting until dark, to avoid meeting people who might have read about Paul. But postponing collecting the day's delivery only raised my anxiety. Sylvia told me she thought I was "wearing my husband's shame." She reminded me that I hadn't assaulted anyone or shot anything. I told her I had been focused on what my neighbors knew. I was also aware my thoughts were irrational. I practiced some cognitive-behavioral techniques and began to go to my mailbox with my head held high. Paul didn't choose mental illness either.

Besides the IRS and attorney bills, Paul's hospital bills began to arrive six months after his shoulder surgeries. I called the hospital regarding insurance and my HMO. I was told to inform my school district about my divorce in progress. Paul would be ineligible for benefits when the divorce was final. I was told by my district to send Paul the bills. I had no idea how he'd pay for anything with no current employment. Occasionally, we heard rumors from family and friends about where he might be living. He certainly didn't seem to have a permanent address.

February 2, 1995, was Groundhog Day, and pretty dismal and gray outside. I decided to get my mail. A new bill came from my attorney. Legal terms like "discovery" and "prove-ups" meant more billable hours plus more court visits. However, despite the gray day, tucked inside the bill was a letter with the good news about a final divorce court date. I felt the day lighten. I would soon see the end to this chapter of my life.

March 21 came quickly: the Judgment for the Dissolution of Marriage Day. I couldn't believe we would finally meet in court to legally end our marriage. The process had taken so long.

Paul had not attended any of our other court proceedings during his jail sentence. I didn't recognize him as he walked in the hallway outside the courtroom. It had been eleven months since I had seen him. He had lost a lot of weight and avoided looking at me. We filed into the courtroom, and Paul sat down next to me. This was the man I had known and loved for over thirty-two years and now he looked like a common stranger. The man I had loved and married had disappeared. This felt like a death. A new man had taken over, and I didn't know him. What I had read about him, I hardly believed. Paul tried making small talk about the kids. I heard myself talking as though nothing had changed. We could have been talking about our shopping list for the week. This felt surreal. I thought about running away, but I was also curious about what he would say.

The judge called our names. Our attorneys prompted us up to the judge's bench. We were both asked basic yes -or -no questions. I remember the serious tone of the men, but not the actual words. Paul and I didn't look at each other. It would have been too painful for me, but I had no idea what he was feeling. It felt as though I were watching a movie starring other people. The gavel came down and we were pronounced divorced. It was all in a day's work for the judge. It ended our married life. It ended the hopes and dreams of our future. It ended my fantasies of being grandparents and enjoying our grandchildren someday.

My attorney fees and costs totaled over $15,000 and it wasn't a contested divorce. I have no idea what it might have cost had we gone to trial. It cost both our children far more.

CHAPTER 33

Avoiding Foreclosure and the Home Inspector

In early June 1995, Max graduated from high school. We were both happy the day had arrived. There wasn't a parent at the ceremony any prouder than I was of my son. He had a very successful high school career despite all of the hardships he'd endured. I clapped louder than most parents in the bleachers since I had to clap for two people. Paul's sister had reported that Paul had been arrested in another part of the state. If he hadn't been ill and in jail, he would have been clapping very hard, too.

By the middle of June 1995, my two tenants were evicted. On July 1 Max and I arrived at "this old house" to prepare for the volunteers Pastor Don had recruited. We arrived at 7:45 a.m., blowing up balloons so the twelve church members could identify the house. Volunteers began arriving at 8:00 a.m. Cars kept pouring into our driveway. Some were people we had never met. They dove into some very messy jobs. One older lady lined the cupboards while her husband scraped and waterproofed the basement walls. I had never met this couple before. What magnificent people. The crew pruned trees, painted, scrubbed and hammered. I served as coordinator, insuring each person had a job with the necessary tools.

I made a run to the hardware store for new panes of glass. As I returned to the house, I stopped at the "Y" fork in the road, waiting to make a left-hand turn into the driveway. The driver behind me failed to see my turn signal and drove right into the back of my car. I was snapped back and forth despite my seatbelt. I thought about my new glass panes on the back seat. I'd heard breaking glass, which turned out to be the turn signal light and car window. My glass panes were intact. The back half of my car had been crumbled in a matter of seconds. The driver of the Chevy Blazer that struck my car approached me, admitting it was his fault for not noticing me in time. The police were called and he was issued a ticket.

Max crossed the street to see what happened. He held me. I was shaking. Then Pastor Don came over. I cried a little. My head hurt and I felt dizzy. I went back to work on the house, trying to forget about the car. We all ate pizza someone had ordered while I was getting the new glass. Both the house and yard looked100 percent better.

Ann and Jason arrived later in the day and insisted I go to the ER. I went and was given a prescription for pills to ease the pain from the whiplash. The doctor recommended ice packs and two days of bed rest. That evening, one of our church volunteers sent over a beautiful garden bouquet. I photographed them. I felt blessed, despite the accident. What a day.

Three days later on the fourth of July, I turned 49. I was grateful to be on the planet with my children. Among the blessings I counted were a good father, wonderful step-mother and good friends. I'd outlived my mom, who died at age forty-eight. I was also grateful she didn't have to witness my life in tatters now.

Paul's affairs didn't directly impact me any longer, but I had read about him in the paper the day after my birthday. He was being charged with a Class 4 felony for criminal damage to property, a truck and a trailer. He was ordered to spend another week in jail; he had missed appointments with his probation officer. Bond was set at $76,000.

I should have been beyond the point of being shocked or surprised. But I thought about the contrast between the man I read about and the one I married when I was twenty-two. They didn't seem like the same person. The Paul I married would be appalled at the behavior of this new Paul. Neither of our mothers would believe it either. A part of me felt grateful they didn't have to see what had happened to him. How would they have comprehended this odd mixture of possible bipolar disorder and alcoholism that had overtaken him?

Three weeks later, on July 23, our church's choir director offered to help me landscape the rental property to help it sell and avoid foreclosure. Katie was one of the most energetic women I've ever known, the mother of three and also the owner of a landscape business. She confided that her energy source was her bipolar disorder. She claimed she was faithful to her "meds" and so it was under control. What a difference it made when a person got the right help for bipolar disorder.

September first was the designated foreclosure date. Time was critical. Katie was willing to help me make the property look special to attract a buyer in a very short time. She offered to charge me only wholesale cost of materials and donate her advice and labor. Twice she and her daughter Jane brought a pick-up truck loaded with mulch to the house. She told me she delivered "three yards." Max, Katie, Jane and I shoveled, raked and scooped for several hours. We planted flowers and shrubs and pulled weeds. The yard looked beautiful.

I hoped to get an offer. I tried to stay positive in my outlook by reading Dr. Norman Vincent Peale, Deepak Chopra and Wayne Dyer. While I waited for an offer, Katie told me she was getting a divorce. She didn't offer anymore information and I didn't ask. I wondered to myself if her husband was having difficulty with her bipolar disorder. She seemed such a gifted, caring person and mother. Although I could speculate, I couldn't draw any conclusions from outside their relationship. I felt sad for her. And yet in her worst moments, she was helping me avoid foreclosure.

I received an offer on the house, but it disappeared as quickly as it had come in. Needless to say, I was disappointed. A second offer came and again disappeared. My loan payment was overdue, as was the grace period granted by the bank. I begged my banker for time and I was surprised that he granted it. He didn't want the bank to take the home if a sale could be worked out.

That month, Max had hernia surgery and the bill came in before his recovery was complete. I hoped the HMO would take care of part of the $3000 bill. The carpet installers who replaced the carpeting in the rental house wanted their $2000 right away. The home inspector told me the furnace and wiring in the home didn't meet code. The bank wouldn't accept my attorney's assertion that I no longer owned the last farm Paul purchased. They wanted to restructure the loan. I instructed my attorney to direct the bank to sell the property. I was thankful both my father and Max's godfather were patient men, waiting for me to repay my loans for the down payment on our townhouse.

My realtor phoned soon after the bills began arriving.

"I have a third offer on your house," she said. "It seems pretty reasonable, but they'd like to meet you on the property tonight at 7:00 p.m. and bring a home inspector with them. They are also bringing their buyer's agent and the wife's father, who just recovered from a heart attack."

"I'll be there at 6:45 p.m. to turn on lights and sweep the sidewalks," I said. My heart lifted. Maybe this would be the night. Maybe these would be the buyers. I eagerly opened the front door to the customers at 7:05 p.m. The buyer's agent introduced me to the couple and the wife's father. The home inspector ignored my outstretched hand and dispensed with introductions. He pointed his index finger at the far back corner of the kitchen and announced in a gruff voice,

"This house isn't level. You can see with the naked eye that it was built on a slant," he bellowed.

I didn't feel this was an auspicious beginning. I wished we could start over.

I wasn't sure how to follow this comment since I had no proof to the contrary. He told the couple and the older gentleman to follow him into the basement. He seemed to know where to go without asking for any guidance from me. I stayed in the kitchen, but could hear the home inspector's voice over the others.

"As you can see, this basement has suffered from considerable water damage. I can see the watermarks," he continued.

My realtor spoke up. "As a matter of fact, sir, I would disagree. We've had this home listed for several months throughout one of the rainiest seasons ever recorded for this area. I came out after every major storm and there was no trace of water at all. This is a very dry basement."

"Well, ma'am, I hate to disagree, but I'd say we have a problem here."

All of a sudden, the older gentleman said to the inspector, "My daughter and her husband like this house. The property looks like a park. I think you are a troublemaker, Mr. Home Inspector, and we don't think you're being honest here. I don't see any evidence of water damage like you say."

I was still in the kitchen, but I could hear Mr. Home Inspector's voice and the heart attack survivor's voice both becoming more strident.

Soon I heard the wife say, "Dad, put your arms down. Making a fist in your condition is not what you need now. Think about your doctor's advice and stay calm. Maybe it was too early for you to leave the hospital. We probably shouldn't have brought you here tonight."

Not deterred, Mr. Home Inspector continued, "As long as we're on the subject of water, did you happen to notice there were no gutters or downspouts on the home? Let's go outside and I'll show you."

I heard the footsteps tromp upstairs and mumbling, which I failed to decipher. They all walked past me and went outdoors.

I heard the elderly gentleman erupt with "You jackass, home inspector. What do you call these gutters and downspouts? I don't believe one vile word out of your mouth tonight. You haven't been honest with us." At that comment, the home inspector decided to leave. As he handed me his card, he said, "Listen, if you ever need to hire a home inspector, give me a call."

His daughter nodded her head and said, "My husband and I really like this house and the location is perfect for our work. We'll be happy to sit down with our agent and your realtor tomorrow and sign the contract at your asking price."

I saw my realtor wink at me as she walked out the door. We were both quite surprised the homebuyers were not dissuaded by the home inspector. I had a signed contract the next day and my foreclosure worries were over.

CHAPTER 34

A Farm Sale and Financial Triumph

My hometown attorney called me, not to be confused with my divorce attorney. This was the attorney who was charged with untangling the state of our farm affairs. Max and I drove to his office. He advised me that he had found a buyer for the original farm we owned, and in a relatively short time, it would be sold.

I asked, "Will I end up with any money at all at the end of this sale?"

"No, you won't," he replied. "But you should be grateful not to owe anything. After the sale and taking my percentage of the proceeds, you should break even."

"Well, I guess that's something. I appreciate your having found a buyer. Did you get only one offer?"

"Yes, and I think you were lucky, considering today's economy. The offer is from someone who has solid financial backing and I don't foresee any difficulties. They're a well-known family in the area."

"If a better offer came in, could we still entertain the new offer? I mean, nothing is final until the papers are all drawn, right?"

"Well, theoretically, I suppose we could, but I've told this party that we would be closing in a matter of a few days."

"I may be overly optimistic, but I'd like to see if I can find another offer out there before we close," I said.

"I wouldn't hold out false hopes or discourage the offer you have on the table now," he admonished.

"Perhaps you're right, but I'd like a few days before we do anything final," I said. "Thank you for all you've done."

I picked my purse up from the floor and left through the waiting room to let Max know we were finished. On our way home, I told Max about my plan to find another bidder for the remaining farm.

"You don't have much time, Mom. This could be our only offer."

"You're right. It could be. But I'm going to advertise our farm. I'm going to buy some blank index cards and post a short description with our phone number in all the towns we pass on our way home. We'll tack them up at grocery stores, convenience stores and local pubs. When we get home, I'll contact the local newspapers and shopping guides and advertise some more. It won't cost much and it can't hurt. Will you help me?"

"Sure, Mom. We have nothing to lose."

Thus, we began tacking up our little homemade cards in every small town we crossed on the highway leading home.

About a week later I received a call.

"I'd like to speak to the party advertising an eighty- acre farm for sale in L. County," the voice said.

"I am the party," I said. "How can I help you?"

"I don't know if you've lined up any other offers, but I'm prepared to offer you six-hundred and twenty-five dollars per acre for that plot. I have a farm tangent to yours and I'd like to expand what I currently have."

I quickly compared his offer to the one on my attorney's table and decided this would give me a profit of about $50,000 instead of no profit.

"I'll give you the phone number for my attorney. He'll draw up the necessary papers. I don't think there will be a problem. We are looking to close very quickly and there is another offer out there, but I'll let my attorney know we've spoken and I'm accepting your offer over the existing one."

I called my attorney and told him the news. He wasn't happy at all. He felt we should go with the original offer.

Despite my attorney's objections, we closed in two weeks and I received a check for $45,000. This enabled me to pay off some debts, buy Max a new truck to take to the university and help with his tuition.

I felt great. Thanks be to God!

CHAPTER 35

Women and Strange Tales

I believe the observance of the birth of Christ is the most important message at Christmas, but it is so intertwined with the festivity of family, friends, parties and gift giving, it becomes complicated. I hoped I was up for it.

One of Paul's aunts invited Max to join their family for dinner on Christmas. Max was surprised she hadn't included me. He declined the invitation and told her he wouldn't celebrate Christmas with them if I was excluded. I was grateful for his loyalty. I'm not sure I could have handled Christmas alone.

During the next several months, Max, Ann and I would hear from friends concerning Paul's whereabouts. Most stories involved sightings in tents and campgrounds. Once in awhile we would hear he'd been arrested again. Many arrests were related to DUIs, but one was more unusual. A mutual friend and teaching colleague told us Paul had been arrested in a distant county for digging fiber optic cable to use as a clothesline.

One day about a year after our divorce, I received a phone call from a woman named Cheryl. The conversation began, "You don't know me, but I am engaged to your ex-husband and he has broken my heart. I've allowed him to move in with my two sons and me. But one of my sons has run away from home because of Paul. They got into a terrible fight. Is there something wrong with him? Is he crazy or an alcoholic or something? I need to know."

I said, "First, Cheryl, I'm not sure how you got my number, although I have some theories. Second, I don't know you or anything about your particular situation other than what you've disclosed. I would advise you to seek counseling and take good care of yourself and your sons. I can't comment on my former husband's mental status. Take good care of yourself." She began sobbing and hung up. I sat by my phone and stared at it. Never in a million years would I have thought I'd have a conversation like that one.

I decided to focus on the most recent good news. Jason had graduated from college with his bachelor's degree in economics. His parents had moved to a large city and there were many opportunities for Jason as well. Although I was excited for them, I was very sad to see Ann and Jason move farther away. They quickly found a lot on which to build their first home. I couldn't wait to visit them.

Ann had visited a university and discovered it had a beautiful campus. She suggested Max consider it. She claimed there were a lot of "granola boys" like Max there. Her term of endearment referred to his habits of healthy eating and working out. Max had decided to spend his first college year living at home and commuting to a nearby community college. But it was good to think about future plans. Max liked the idea of attending the university, but only after completing a year in a community college. He might be able to qualify for in-state tuition and attend the university his final two years. He now had a goal and a plan. Max started his freshman year thinking he wanted to be a business major. He switched to human biology. This would prove to make a big difference in his life.

Ann began receiving letters from her dad. The letters now had a different flavor since our divorce. The first letters had had a bitter tone. He had returned her high school senior portraits to her, saying she was no longer his daughter. These painful letters were now replaced with "newsy" letters. Initially, he talked about dating different women and being happy again. He was excited because a school district in Iowa had failed to trace his felony convictions and he was teaching in a high school. The downside: he was abruptly fired through no fault of his own. He'd had an argument with an administrator and he wasn't about to back down. The next letters were more somber. He was homeless again, living in a campground. He was suspicious of the cops in Iowa. He was being unfairly arrested again. The letters came sporadically, but were dismal overall.

One day, Ann received one that sounded jubilant, if not euphoric. He talked about his new wife, Dina. A few days after Ann received this celebratory letter, I received a phone call from Dina.

"Hello, Carol. You don't know me, but my name is Dina. I married your ex-husband four days ago (this was in the late 1990s) and I'm about to file for divorce. He beat me up last night and I have a few broken ribs and two black eyes. What is wrong with him? Is he crazy or something? I don't get him. We met in AA and I thought he was so good-looking and nice. I can't believe this happened to me. I'd like an explanation."

I repeated the same refrain I had given his former fiancée, Cheryl. "Well, Dina, I'd encourage you to get help for yourself. It sounds like you could use the help of a professional therapist. Get to a safe place first. I can't explain my former husband's behavior. Please take care of yourself right now."

I heard sobbing in the background. It reminded me of Cheryl's crying a few months before. Dina hung up. Paul seemed to be handing out my phone number to women he had hurt. It was time to get that changed.

I felt sad for both of these women. They had evidently invested their hopes and dreams in Paul, only to have them destroyed soon after. I hoped they would get help and grow stronger before falling for his or anyone else's false promises. Other than cautioning them to be careful, I felt helpless. I didn't know Paul's current psychological condition or legal status firsthand. But it didn't sound like he was showing signs of improvement. In fact, they both seemed to have suffered more violence in their short relationships than I had in my long one with him. It sounded as though his violent behaviors were escalating. Was he still running from the law? It was good to hear he'd been attending AA meetings.

A month later, Ann received a phone call from her Aunt Jan, Paul's sister. Paul had been arrested and put in jail. Evidently, his new wife Dina had needed surgery for a brain tumor. When she returned home, her head was wrapped in a turban to cover her head, which had been shaven prior to surgery. Paul became distraught. This may have triggered his own memories of his father's brain tumor surgeries when he was a child. Paul unleashed his anger on Dina, broke several ribs and gave her multiple bruises. Dina had returned to the hospital to recover from her latest Paul-inflicted injuries. Paul was serving time in jail.

Ann received a letter from her father a month later. Paul had been released from jail, but fell from a roof trying to save a cat. He was recovering from his injuries in the hospital. Ann decided to call her Aunt Jan to find out if she knew more.

"Ann, I'm not so sure about the story of your dad falling off the roof trying to save a cat. I heard that Paul had actually been run off the road by Dina's brothers. They had vowed revenge for her injuries. He's in St. Luke's Hospital recovering. But I doubt it involved a cat," said Aunt Jan.

Ann called me asking for suggestions about what she should do. I told her I had no way to intervene as a former wife, but as his daughter, she might be able to exert some influence at the hospital. I suggested she work with a social worker there and request an alcohol/psychological assessment be done. Ann made the request and the social worker arranged for a nurse to implement. The nurse, however, decided Paul "didn't look like an alcoholic or fit the profile" so she abandoned the assessment. Evidently, there was no attempt to discover his criminal background.

CHAPTER 36

Toads and Tornadoes

August 3, 1997, was such a hot Sunday. A toad hopped up to my front door after a powerful electrical storm blew through. I'm not sure why, but it made me laugh.

I had been legally divorced for two and a half years by this time. I hosted brunch for five divorced lady friends. I wanted them to meet my new roommate, Janet. I stayed up late Saturday night to prepare the dishes and set a pretty table.

Max had come home for a week-long visit, taking a break before the next fall semester began. He planned to go camping for a few days with some old high school buddies and spend the remainder of time with me. Ann had worked out a break in her schedule to visit at the same time. It was great to have her home with me.

The visit passed quickly and Max packed to return to college as a full-time student and said his good-bys before I was ready. Maybe it was why I wanted to keep so busy, so I wouldn't have to think about him leaving. It was so good to see him this past week. Max had had a great time camping and canoeing with his friend in the Sylvania Wilderness. I laughed at his story of the squirrel eating their oatmeal and the field mouse he found sitting in his chicken noodle soup. I was so glad they had a good time.

Four out of five of my divorced friends claimed to be "in love." I told them sometimes you have to kiss a lot of toads before the prince comes. The group advised me *I didn't have to kiss them all.* One friend repeated that now familiar refrain, "Good judgment comes from experience and experience comes from bad judgment."

I called Max at 10:30 p.m. to see if he had made it home safely. His arrival was planned for 9:00 p.m. His roommate answered. (I was still getting used to the fact his roommate was Cheri and not a guy. He wasn't dating her. It was a good rent- splitting arrangement. I felt very old- fashioned.) He hadn't arrived yet. I was worried.

At midnight Max called. He had encountered a tornado when he crossed the bridge into Iowa. An RV ahead of him was picked up into the air and spun around. It was then pushed into the ground by a ferocious wind. The expressway signs were ripped out of the ground and flew across the expressway. Another RV spiraled into the ditch ahead of him. There had been one fatality. Max sounded shaken. He'd seen hail the size of marbles.

"Mom, I'm worried about the finish on my new truck."

"Max, forget the damned truck. You're alive. That's all that matters."

CHAPTER 37

Therapy for the Therapist

I'd been divorced for almost three and a half years. I had a strong relationship with both of my children again. I took pride in the townhouse I owned through the help of my dad and Max's godfather. I no longer needed an order of protection. I was not living in fear and felt in good physical health. I had lost about twenty-five pounds doing step aerobics and was more physically fit than I was in my thirties. Although I was fifty-two, I felt like twenty-two. I slept soundly and the kids and I were alive. I was amazed at how well they weathered the storm, but they were not without scars. Our children are the best of both of us. I will be forever proud of them. We survived.

As I reflected on my life as a married woman I was baffled by the mystery of our marriage. The man I thought I knew for most of my life I didn't know by the end of our marriage. I often wondered at what point I had stopped knowing him. At what point had he stopped confiding in me? At what point had he mentally and emotionally vacated the life I thought we were still sharing? When did my reality become fiction?

I dated some men, one quite seriously, who proposed marriage. But I wasn't ready, and wondered if I ever would be. It wouldn't be fair to either of us until I was in a more settled place within myself. I could tell I wasn't over my grieving when my concentration was intermittent. My short- term memory was not as keen. For instance, I could find myself putting a gallon of milk in the pantry and then catching myself, because I was thinking of other things. I called someone on the phone and heard it ringing and forgot who I was calling or what I was calling about. My mind was often too crowded to think clearly. There seemed to be some fact I was searching for, a missing puzzle piece. If I could just find that missing piece that teased me at the periphery of my brain, I might solve the puzzle. And the ultimate question I asked myself was, "Why?" There was no simple answer. The world is imperfect. We humans are imperfect. But my faith and the grace of God helped our family survive it. Those were the answers I ended with.

I eventually found a therapist. Given the nature of my profession and my strong belief in the power and benefits of psychotherapy, it should have been an immediate priority. But I knew a lot of the therapists in my region as friends and acquaintances. I needed to find the right one, preferably in another town.

A friend of mine had been a client of a clinical psychologist for some time. Since she was also a therapist I trusted her assessment. I decided to make an appointment with him. He was helpful beyond my expectations. His approach was a good match to my needs and he diagnosed me with post- traumatic stress disorder. I was surprised by this diagnosis since I hadn't been a military survivor of war or physically battered. But it did make sense to me after I thought about it. After seeing him for a few months, I felt a weight lift and my mood brighten. I fell asleep faster.

I began to see myself as a strong survivor. I had lost my husband to mental illness and alcoholism. I had lost three farms, two homes and all of our savings. I'd sold antiques to buy food. I'd paid off $10,000 worth of credit card debt and $6,000 in back taxes. I'd bought a townhouse in a safe neighborhood for my son and me to live in. I had launched Max into college. My daughter and her husband were in their first home and growing to love their new state.

Many things triggered my fragmented recollections: black Standard Poodles, riding lawn mowers, Toyota trucks, guns, farms, baptisms, children's sermons, Christmas trees and July 20 (our anniversary date). So many little memories caught me off guard, land mines in a field waiting for detonation. I began to distrust the pleasant memories and question their validity. They only served to remind me of what could be no more.

Children have a way of keeping you focused on the present. In this case, it was good news because Max had met the woman of his dreams and they decided to get married over the Memorial Day weekend in 2001. May 26 proved to be a gorgeous day and the wedding was a beautiful event. I loved his choice for a bride. Hannah was a beautiful Christian woman from a close-knit family. I was happy for Max. I was *not* comfortable with Max's dad coming to the wedding and possibly disrupting the day. I was still afraid of him, but also fearful of what he could do at a wedding with so much importance for all of us. Our last encounter alone together had been laced with threats, and I had powerful flashbacks to those moments. I told Max of my reservations and he honored my request not to include him. I know I added to Max's pain on that day, but I felt strongly that the wedding needed to be about Max and Hannah, not about Max's dad or my fears.

The fall of 2001 was filled with both immense joy and grief. Tragedy befell our nation at the towers of the New York World Trade Center, the Pentagon and the field in Pennsylvania on 9/11. It was catastrophic. I will never forget attending the in-service at my school on new computer programs and hearing an announcement about a plane flying into the first tower. I remember looking at the video replay with my fellow teachers and counselors in disbelief.

During the fall season of 2001, Ann and Jason had a late night visitor drive up on a motorcycle to their new home. Paul needed food and shelter and had no where else to go.

Ann called me and explained, "Mom, I have to help out Dad. He'd help me if I were in desperate straits. If the shoe were on the other foot, I know he'd take care of me."

"Honey, you do whatever you choose, but you don't have an obligation to provide him with room and board."

"Well, it won't be forever. He needs to stay with us until he gets back on his feet. He'll find a job and then move out."

"It might be a good idea to put some boundaries around your hospitality. You and Jason might discuss this and come up with a plan you're both comfortable with."

"Yeah, we already talked about doing that. It's not like we want him living with us forever."

"That's good. I wish you well. I think it is very good of you to offer your help and home."

This temporary arrangement lasted through Ann and Jason's move to another state. Paul lived with them through a variety of jobs. During the latter portion of his stay, he and Ann began a joint business venture. They worked on remodeling homes, building decks, painting and plumbing. Ann helped her dad during the hours she wasn't involved in managing a retail store. She had a demanding full- time job and her weekends were devoted to helping Paul with various renovation projects. She was often exhausted, but didn't complain. Paul and Jason were getting along well for some time and the arrangement seemed to be working better than anticipated.

CHAPTER 38

New Beginnings at Middle Age

Just over a month later, on November 17, I called my son to wish him a happy birthday. I could hardly imagine he was already twenty-five. I was proud of his accomplishments. He'd begun work on his master's degree after getting his B.S. degree in human biology.

On the same evening, I met a man I had written to on Match. com. I had become very discouraged about dating at the age of 55. I was hoping I would someday be in a healthy relationship, but had no desire to repeat the mistakes of my past. I met John for dinner. I had my own car; I wanted to be able to leave the scene and disappear to my home without a trace if the evening didn't go well—but it did. Meeting John gave me hope that things could get better.

John had also been divorced. He was an accountant. We both had an elder daughter and younger son. Their ages were all within a year of each other. John was six months younger than me. We had both been brought up Catholic, but were no longer practicing. Our fathers had both suffered from alcoholism and had been purchasing managers for their respective companies. They had both served in WWII and had even been stationed at the same camp. John lived across the street from my cousin who he referred to as my "eye in the sky."

We enjoyed a lot of the same things. I found I could accept his passions, football and photography. (I had dated a ham radio operator and kite flyer, an antique collector, a bullet maker, a psychology teacher, a pilot and a wealthy man who wanted to travel with me but couldn't be relied on for the truth. They had all lead to dead ends.) John and I were both skittish about commitment and wanted to take our time. We began dating steadily, taking our time to learn about each other. Neither of us wanted to rush headlong into a mistake we'd regret.

Eventually, things in my daughter's home began to unravel. An inventory of the liquor cabinet revealed a lot of water had been added to the alcohol being stored and it was all diluted. Phone calls started coming in from disgruntled customers complaining about jobs started but not finished. Some customers called to say Paul hadn't shown up to start a job he'd taken on. Ann and Jason knew they needed to confront him and they were not looking forward to it. Paul was putting a strain on their marriage by this point, and things needed to change.

And everything did during the Christmas season in 2003. Ann and Jason found discrepancies in Paul's stories regarding his work with customers. Although I wasn't present at the final confrontation, Ann told me the conversation got heated. She and Jason told Paul he needed to leave their home.

I told her later, "You and Jason did an awesome job helping your dad in every way you could. You helped him to find work for two years and gave him room and board. I'm so proud of you, but I also understand your frustration."

"Mom, we tried so hard, but Dad wouldn't follow any rules and we couldn't trust him."

"I know, honey. Putting alcohol with bipolar disorder creates quite a train wreck if it's not dealt with."

"I learned a lot from Dad in the process, though. I can rip out a toilet and have it on my driveway in fifteen minutes. I can pop an eight -foot long mirror off a wall and put up a new one. I can do a lot of handyman jobs I never knew how to do before. I've also decided to go back to school. I plan to be a social worker."

"That's amazing. You'd make a terrific one. I'll support your decision, but I 'm surprised you're thinking of leaving retail management after all these years. I can also understand it. Your hours have always been horrendous and it has never been easy work."

"It won't be quick, since I have to finish my bachelor's degree first and then get my master's, but I'm looking for a change and this seems to be the time."

"I wish you the best, honey. Keep me posted."

On New Year's Day, 2004, John proposed and I happily accepted. We planned a small outdoor wedding for July, with our family members in a Japanese garden located in a forest preserve. My nephew, an ordained Lutheran minister, agreed to perform the ceremony. Our four adult children would meet for the first time on the day of the wedding. They were all married and they all suggested if we needed marital advice, we "newlyweds" could come to them anytime. I hired a violin quartet from my high school to provide the music.

It rained on the morning of the wedding. We didn't have a backup plan. There were some picnic shelters close to the garden, but I hadn't paid much attention to tables covered in bird dirt. We hoped for the best and by afternoon the rain had stopped. The skies were bright blue and the temperature comfortable. We had been blessed from on high. The wedding was beautiful and the reception dinner at a local Italian restaurant was very enjoyable. We couldn't have asked for a more elegant and simple ceremony. We had both endured so much loss in our lives, we were joyful.

Cake and ice cream followed at our new townhouse. We were both so happy to be moving forward with our lives and launching into our futures together.

John and I started thinking seriously about retirement in two years. We had just gone through the arduous task of building the townhouse to our specifications for the two years we planned to live there and finish out our careers. We were looking beyond the Midwest and decided we would move out of state and enjoy the Southwest, where we wouldn't have to confront snow and ice anymore.

By July 2005, our first granddaughter was born, weighing only 2 pounds and 9 ounces. She was a C-section baby and at very high risk. The baby and her mother, John's daughter, had to stay in the hospital for a long time. Our little granddaughter was a fighter and survived, despite the odds. I saw life coming faster now, with four children between us and the promise of more grandchildren on the way.

Max and Hannah lived an hour way from us, but we doubted they would stay in my home state forever. Max was now a physician's assistant and had a promising future. So the chances of them moving someday were high. We knew we couldn't follow our four children around the country wherever their jobs took them. We decided to tell them of our plans to retire to the Southwest. This came as a shock to them, but they accepted it as well as they could be expected to. We would be working on the plans of our new home from a distance, with occasional trips to the new building site to track the progress of our retirement home.

In January 2006, our second granddaughter was born to Max and Hannah. John beat me to the hospital to visit our newest, Ava. She was full term and normal weight. She, too, was strong. We felt blessed to be able to share in such good news for our family.

CHAPTER 39

MIA No Longer

John and I retired to Arizona in June of 2006. We loved our new, low-maintenance retirement home. We loved the idea of exploring such a beautiful state with so many interesting landmarks and history. Our first year was spent decorating and completing the landscaping. Learning about how we were going to spend our retirement years was a big transition for us. The first year passed quickly.

We both missed seeing our children and new grandchildren. I eagerly accepted an invitation to visit my children the following year. Ann and Max greeted me at the airport in St. Louis on December 20, 2007. I was invited to spend a few days before Christmas with them, their spouses and Ava.

I told them, "I should fly home before the 24th. Because John and I are hosting a Christmas Eve party for our neighbors," I explained. "But," I continued, "it feels so right to be here with you both. I'm so excited."

Three days at Ann and Jason's house flew by too fast. Ann had gotten leopard print pajamas for Max's wife Hannah, herself and me. She completed our outfits with matching red socks, echoing the red trim on the pajamas. We looked so funny, we laughed. Ava was delightful at almost one year. We reconnected easily, despite the long months since I had last seen her. She cried when I said good-by. I love living in the Southwest with my husband, but both of us missed our families and wished they were closer.

Jason was supportive and maintained two jobs to help replace her loss of income and maintain their current lifestyle. It was stressful and demanding for both of them.

On December 29, 2007, Ann called. Jason had located Paul who has been a missing person for three years. His last conversation with Ann and Max ended with him telling them neither would see him again. Max had assumed he was dead. Ann didn't know, but feared any new news wouldn't be good. Evidently, he was released from the state mental facility several days before Ann started her MSW internship there. He served a three-year sentence for aggravated DWI and bad check writing. He had been released to a nearby work release program. Ann kept her sense of humor. She said she was relieved he would not be a participant in her small group.

I spoke to Max the following day. He said the news was better than he anticipated; he had assumed his dad was dead by this time.

"Well, Max, it's good to know he's being monitored, fed and sheltered," I said.

"Yeah. It's not nearly as final as being dead."

Without input from family members, Paul's self-report and criminal history would be the only source of information available for the professionals working with him. The alcohol abuse/ dependency might be obvious to them. But would anyone take the time to look further into the possibility of bipolar disorder as the source of his need to self-medicate?

CHAPTER 40

Have you been in the Pool?

By May 2008, John and I felt very settled into our new place, which felt like a resort. Our children, grandchildren and neighbors provided great joy to our lives. We loved living in our, low- maintenance, beautiful home where a golf cart served as our second car.

I was teaching water fitness, as well as swimming laps, golfing and practicing yoga. I experienced both the pain and pleasure of two major acting roles in our local theater.

John supported my efforts to surpass my comfort zone and try new challenges while he enjoyed photography, golf and watching his favorite football team, the Green Bay Packers. Our many blessings illustrated how life can change from very stressful to very satisfying.

I had never envisioned a future this fulfilling when I was going through the terrifying end of my first marriage. I was happy to have made the choice to continue life and not to have given in to my suicidal fantasies in my darkest moments. I prayed for my former husband. The children and I understood he was ill. We prayed someday he'd be healthy and whole again, living a more satisfying and meaningful life. I hoped he could reconnect with the kids and have a healthy relationship with them someday.

Max, Hannah and little Ava moved to another state and Max took a new position in September 2008. They closed on a new home on September 10th. John and I were very happy for them.

Ann and Max received letters from Paul, who explained to them he was in an alcohol recovery and work release program. Paul learned about the death of his younger brother in January 2007 and that he inherited substantial money from him. However, there were complications. The state had some ownership because of his incarceration. He wanted the kids involved in some decision -making regarding the inheritance. They worked with an attorney to find the best possible solution for their dad. It was a positive step. He was finally getting some help. It had taken fourteen years.

November 1, 2008 was the day Ann and Max decided to go visit their dad. Ann was thirty-six and Max was about to turn thirty-two. It had been six years since Max has seen his dad and about four years for Ann. They weren't sure which work release facility or mission he was staying in, but decided to join together on their quest to find him. I was proud of them and prayed the visit would go well.

After they found the Department of Corrections facility, they were allowed to leave with their dad and go somewhere for a bite to eat. They said the visit went well and there was a spirit of optimism about Paul's future. He would be released in thirty to sixty days and then assigned to one year of probation. He told them he was in a Twelve-Step Program and participating in Bible studies twice a day. I was glad to hear he was interested in seeing Ava for the first time. Max offered to pick him up and bring him to his home for a visit with his wife and Ava, now almost three years old.

The next week was Paul's first visit with Ava. He brought crayons and a coloring book with him to facilitate their time together. Her parents told her she was a lucky girl to have three grandfathers.

The most humorous words were uttered by Ava, as only a child could do. She was in her car seat next to her newly introduced grandfather. As she studied the skin on his sixty-two –year- old hand she asked, "Have you been in the pool … a lot?"

CHAPTER 41

Brutal News (A Year Later)

On December 1, 2009, I received an e-mail from Ann. It read: "Dad was evicted on Max's birthday. (November 17). He is being sued for $2700 worth of property damage, which could be the cleanup fee. I let Max and Hannah know in case he landed at their door." Paul had been living in a cheap apartment building somewhere near his parole office.

Since my children now lived about two hours apart, Paul arriving at Max's to seek lodging was a strong possibility. The kids were in neighboring states, but geographically close. When we visited it made it easy to visit them both.

Long periods of time elapsed between contacts with Paul and the children. It was difficult to know his whereabouts. Ann and Max had grown accustomed over the years to his disappearance, not knowing where he lived or if he was hiding from the law. Sometimes they would find out he had been in jail again.

On Saturday, February 6, 2010, I received another e-mail from Ann. The subject line read, "The ex- husband update":

"I think Dad's in jail again for a DUI he got on my birthday. It looks like he's serving 120 days as of January 11. No wonder he hasn't called recently, asking us to buy him a house. He's in the "big house" and doesn't need one right now. Thank God we didn't give him money to put down on some crack house….It would be vacant and our responsibility at this point. How many times can a person go to jail for DUI without them doing something else to him? I think this one makes number six. Thank God he has not killed anyone yet with a car."

Three days later, I received a phone call from Max. "Mom, I have some sad news. A police officer came to our front door today and I knew right away it wouldn't be good. Dad was found dead on the street this morning. He was downtown, not far from where he was working as a maintenance guy at a 7-11. They're not sure of the cause of death. The police officer said they were going to do an autopsy. It appears he had a heart attack and was transported in an ambulance to an ER. Someone had found him on the street and tried to administer CPR."

I was without words. We had all known this day could come, but when it did, it was still a shock.

"I thought he was in jail, serving some time for a DUI, not working …'

"Yeah, that's how it sounded to Ann and me. But he may have gotten into another work release program. He'd not been speaking to me for awhile. He wasn't happy Ann and I weren't buying him the house he had his heart set on. But neither of us thought he was well enough to own a home."

"I know, honey. It wouldn't have been a good solution to his problems. You and Ann did all you could. You bought him clothes, took him out to eat, brought him to your home to play with Ava. You both tried. No one had the power to keep him from drinking or getting more DUIs. I'm very proud of you both and how you tried to help him."

"Thanks, Mom. Ann and I will talk some more. We want to have some kind of memorial service for him. We're thinking of having him cremated. It's what he wanted, but it will be after we get the autopsy results. I'll keep you posted on what's happening."

"All right. I'm here if you need to talk. How's Hannah doing?"

"Well, she's in shock like the rest of us. But to tell you the truth, we're all a bit relieved he's at peace now. He won't be in pain any more and there's no danger of him hurting anyone else."

"I agree. We can take comfort in that."

After a few days passed, Ann, Max and Hannah were able to gather together at Max's home to plan a local memorial service for the family. Hannah's parents were very active in their church, so they had someone who agreed to help. There were more than a few tears shed by all. Little Ava came over and tried to comfort the adults. "You hug on Aunt Ann, Mom, and I'll hug on Dad. They need to be loved on now," she so wisely said.

The memorial service was scheduled on February 13, a Saturday. I had done plenty of grieving over the past fifteen years, and so my main focus was the kids. They had suffered so much through the years. However, at the service I hadn't expected to see slides of Paul and me on our wedding day. I was twenty-two and he was twenty-one. We looked so young and happy and unaware of our future. I cried and couldn't seem to hold back the tears. I hadn't planned on this, but couldn't stop myself. The reality of what had happened after our beautiful wedding day was too overwhelming. I felt an incredible sadness for Paul, myself and the kids.

I chose him to be their father and felt some anguish over the decision, but they were also the embodiment of all of the good qualities of their father. They wouldn't have become the great adults they were if it weren't for Paul. They had inherited his gifts of intelligence, generosity, creativity, determination and compassion for those less fortunate. And when Paul was well, he had a strong sense of righteousness, representing his teachers' union and serving on his church council. He had been a gifted teacher, farmer and a devoted real estate agent. He'd been a hard-working vocational therapist. He was so many more things than simply a man who had served time in jail for DUIs.

The kids decided to look for the place where Paul last lived. He had actually been living, rent free, in the home he wanted the kids to purchase for him. They went to visit it at the address he had given them and came home as though they'd been jolted with electricity.

"It was far worse than we expected, Mom. He was living in sub-human conditions. He'd been sick. There was no plumbing and he'd used buckets to hold everything. We found a lot of Bibles with notations in the margins. He's been to a lot of Bible classes while staying at the missions. I think he found God again, in his own way, toward the end," said Ann.

"Yeah, if we'd known how bad it was there, we should have got him out of there," Max added. But he didn't tell us how he was living. The place was disgusting. We found eggs lying on shelves in the kitchen. There was no refrigerator. He only wanted us to buy the house, but it wasn't much of a house. There was some kind of written agreement we found between him and the owner. Maybe he was allowed to live in it so no one would break into it. He may have been friends with this guy who owned it. I'm not sure how he knew him. It was a pretty vague arrangement. "We couldn't read the man's last name on the agreement. I'm not sure how he'll find out Dad is dead."

I flew back home on Monday, but knew I'd be flying back again to be with the kids for a second memorial service in Paul's child-hood hometown. He had relatives who weren't able to come to the first service. The next one was scheduled for Saturday, May 15. By then, the ground would be soft in the Midwest and his ashes could be buried. Paul had asked to be laid to rest next to his grandparents in a tiny little churchyard out in the remote countryside. I thought about why he hadn't wanted to be interred next to his parents and brother. I think it was probably because his grandparents had been his physical and emotional anchors when his own nuclear family was adrift in illness and surgeries. Paul had often recounted his fond memories of being on the farm with his grandparents at sowing, summer and harvest time.

CHAPTER 42

The Second Memorial Service

The kids ordered a headstone and invited all of Paul's family to come. A family dinner was to follow the service. Max had written poignant verses for the first memorial service and Ann had made copies for all. They decided to make more copies for this service as well. It was beautifully done and worth sharing.

I felt some apprehension about this second service day. Paul's family members not spoken to me for fifteen years. Did they still blame me? I didn't know, but I also decided at this point I didn't care. I had done my best and I couldn't change their judgment of me. The morning was cool. The old white Catholic church sat by itself in a cornfield with a large cemetery in front of it. It was hard to tell how many farmers and their loved ones were laid to rest here. I focused on little Ava and her new baby brother Brandon at the service.

The service pamphlet read:

In Loving Memory
Paul ....
December 15, 1946-February 9, 2010
Born a farm boy,
Later a farmer.
Became a husband,
Later a father.
Thrust into adulthood
Provider to his family.
Born practical
Later Spiritual.
Lived in suburbia
With his boots in a farm field.
Protector of stray animals,
And hunter of all the rest.

Early morning fisherman,
Late night veterinarian.
Rainy day mechanic,
Spring time landscaper.
Summer time carpenter
Autumn harvester.
Home seller, landlord, homeless.
Husband
Father
Friend.
Loved by many,
He will be missed.

Max didn't sign his name, but family members knew he was the author.

The next page was a poem the kids had discovered written by Paul. I hadn't seen it before. It was written many years after our divorce.

The Wild Ones

I try to stay home, but my feet go walking.
Towards my little wild ones when the dark times fall.
Oh! They talk so as the twilight ends,
Down the darkened wide woody creeks draw,
The black green covers them all except their crying happy sad call.

I try to stay home, but my feet go walking.
Pulled along the dust soft trails to the black oaks of the Ellison's
And westerly then down to where the Deep and the wolf run on.
Following as best I can, the calling songs of my little wild ones.

I cannot stay home. My feet go walking.
The little one's families talk so sweet and high and wild,
As the dark pulls them too,
Up and out to play and hunt and sing
And just BE once more for this nite's while.

I cannot stay home. My feet go walking.
To be unhearing of my little ones would be like
Living life's love song unsung beneath a starless dome.
As if knowing what could be while running so warm and young and strong,
But choosing to sit alone within the cold, cold old walk of my cabin home.

I try to stay home, but my feet go walking.
The black darkness halts my followings now of my little coyote ones.
Their echoed voices fade far west of where the Deep and wolf do run.
Howling over the sandy oakened bluff and
Down toward the Great River's hunting fun.

Just once more, thank God,
I've joined my little ones though they know me not.
Running briefly with them in that grey somewhere.
Our somewhere so far back that both our time's forgot.
I try to stay home, but my feet go walking.

Paul......

The third page of the service was a story I hadn't heard before, which Paul had also written. I have a memory of my family buying a Christmas tree at Paul's home when I was young.

Selling Christmas Trees

For a couple of Christmas times from 1956-1958 we sold Christmas trees at our house. The first year was a fun thing for me; trees and lights in the side yard, plus all the people coming around. When I was in the sixth grade it wasn't fun. Nobody else did that in their yard.

My youngest sister was born in March, so the time Mom used to spend with Dad and the trees became my time to be cold. Mostly it wasn't fun because we needed to sell stuff in our yard.

I was the only one outside in the tree lot. Suppertime was always slow, the poor looking couple from the old college apartment came to look at the trees. Mom called their place a tenement house.

The nice trees were $6.00, the cheapest ones were $1.50 and we had some bad one-sided ones for a dollar. Dad called them "Orphans." We cut them up to make boughs, wreaths and roping. They seemed to look at all the cheaper trees over and over and whispered about prices. I heard money-talk a lot so I didn't pay much attention to the cold price-word whispers. The guy had a $3.00 one all picked out when his thin-faced wife pulled him over to the orphans. She had two orphan Jack pines together so their flat sides touched. They both laid their mittens in the snow and took some pieces of twine string off of the tree stands and used it to tie the two bad trees together. She was real happy with the looks of the new tree and he even smiled a little.

I used to see him almost every day sitting on his apartment porch steps when I walked home from school. He never smiled when I was walking by; some people don't I guess. Now he was smiling with her. He paid me the two bucks with cold reddened hands and picked up their mittens from the snow. She looked some more at the tree and said it was the prettiest one there. Her smile didn't make her pretty, but it made me smile back. For a minute the three of us would have had to have a hundred hearts to be happier. Silly, I suppose kind of what kids feel like sometimes. They started to carry the tree toward the street. I looked at the two one-dollar bills and pushed them deep into my pocket. She even hugged him before they headed toward home. My face now felt warm again.

There always seems to be reasons for me to recall selling trees. Those thoughts change as times go by. Now, I think of what can be made joyful and beautiful by two plain people who willingly lay their mittens in the snow.

Love,
DA (Paul)

The final page chosen for the service was the poem by Veronica Shorffstall, 1971, entitled *Comes theDawn*.

When I returned home I cleaned out a file with many documents left from the time spent writing this book. I found a poem Paul had written and enclosed in some of our long -forgotten financial documents.

* * *

Enjoyed

And in those days past my childhood my joy was born.

I held it in our arms and stood in the many places of our world and in myriad ways shouted to those with hearts to hear "come and stand with us in our sun."

And everyday for moons uncounted, joy was proclaimed in the thousand facets of our world.

Never looking for a shadowing, I then felt the darkened side of trees grown side by each, sharing, then stealing, sun and warmth.

Twas then joy grew pale and weary since no other heart but mine held its loveliness and no other lips kissed its lips.

The freedom joy in sun world days could not just be, not be without diminishment of thee or me.

And now come dead joy days and the reclouded years before its birth.

That life before joy, those years of child's fear and numb sorrows shared by whispers in some memories.

And memory too shall pass away.

It is an autumn leaf that murmurs for a moment in its season's wind and then is heard no more.

Paul

(Readers are welcome to comment about this book on my website: www.bipolarfamilysecret.com. Although I will read them all, I may not be able to respond to all of the messages. My e-mail address is carolhoran@msn.com.)

Final Destination for Too Many: Incarceration of the Mentally Ill

I am a proud National Alliance on Mental Illness (NAMI) member in two states. I am not proud it took me so long to join. As a licensed professional of the healing arts, I should have valued it more as a good resource earlier in my struggles. Due to a combination of false pride and shame, I did not take advantage of their help sooner. Fortunately, many Americans have. I'm heartened to see NAMI's numbers grow.

Some of the facts cited in the fall 2007 *NAMI Advocate* magazine are relevant to this book. The following first four facts are quotes by Angela Kimball, NAMI Director of State Policy (Kimball, *NAMI Advocate*, Fall 2007, p. 7):

Fact 1:

One in four adults—approximately 57.7 million Americans—experiences a mental health disorder in a given year. One in seventeen lives with a serious mental illness, such as schizophrenia, major depression or bipolar disorder, and one in ten children have a serious mental or emotional disorder.

* * *

This fact may be hard for many of us to assimilate. The implications are that this would include many of our family members, fellow coworkers, neighbors, students and friends.

Ronald C. Kessler, the principal investigator for the National Comorbidity Survey, is in the process of conducting a similar survey for adolescents, the first of its kind in the U.S. (Reinhart, Mary K. 2011, May 22).

Traits we once believed were eccentricities might actually be symptoms of a larger problem. Many times people dismiss symptoms of depression, such as irritability or hostility, as major character flaws. Looking the other way and ignoring symptoms can be very costly, as my story illustrates. I was often deceived and I was trained in recognizing symptoms. I had an incredibly hard time believing someone I loved and cared about would suffer from bipolar disorder.

Fact 2:

According to the National Institute of Mental Health, *Mental Illness Exacts Heavy Toll, Beginning in Youth,* June 2005, half of all lifetime cases of mental illness begin by age 14, three-quarters by age 24. Yet, despite the existence of effective treatments, most people go without.

* * *

My former husband was involved in underage drinking while in high school and college. He may have been self-medicating his bipolar disorder while a teenager. At that time in my life, neither he nor I had ever heard of bipolar disorder or manic-depression. Underage drinking was the norm, not the exception, in our high school and college days. Drinking was seen as an adolescent *rite of passage*, nothing more. I had not heard of illegal drug usage during my high school years from 1960-64. The Vietnam War quickly changed that when I graduated from high school.

Despite prevention programs in many of our schools today, both underage drinking and illegal drug use are often viewed as rites of passage for adolescents. I was heavily involved in local and statewide prevention programs in my state, but community norms are very difficult to change.

Fact 3:

Nearly one million adults with mental illness have been homeless. With average disability incomes of 18 percent of the median income, most of these adults cannot afford decent housing.

* * *

During one of my former husband's episodes with homelessness, my daughter and her husband provided him with a beautiful home for a period of two years. My daughter tried to convince her dad that he needed a psychological assessment and counseling. She and her husband did their best to offer him a therapeutic environment, but without the appropriate tools with therapy and medication, it was a doomed attempt at rehabilitation.

Fact 4:

Nearly one in four state prison and local jail inmates has a recent history of a mental health disorder. In our juvenile justice systems, 70 percent of youth have at least one mental disorder.

* * *

During my six years as an outreach family therapist in two counties, funded by a statewide grant, I encountered many chronic truants and potential dropouts. We defined chronic truants as those students who missed 10 percent of the previous 180 school days. Our program did not include students suffering from a truly debilitating physical illness or injury and receiving educational services. It was amazing to me how many students in my caseload suffered from one or more mental disorders. Many of them were dually diagnosed, suffering from both a mental disorder and a substance abuse problem. I was able to help some of them get treatment, outpatient therapy or psychiatric hospitalization. But for many, there was no help available and these students often dropped out of school with no marketable skills. This is alarming when one thinks about the number of young people in our communities who need basic food, shelter and clothing, but have no legal means for supporting these needs.

Some students I worked with had parents who asked me to have the state take care of them. Some of these parents expressed anger and frustration when I told them the state couldn't take care of their children; it already had too many children in the foster care system. I often felt discouraged about the sheer magnitude of the problem. It was very rewarding, however, when a student returned to school and received a diploma later.

According to the National Alliance on Mental Illness, "over five times as many people with mental illness are in jails and prisons than in hospitals." (Kimball, 2007) As appalling as that statistic seems, the part that I find even more alarming is that my former husband was not only arrested and put in jail, but that this event was repeated for a variety of escalating crimes over a sixteen -year period. Not only was he not getting help to become a contributing member of society again, he was provided the tools to become a more experienced criminal. He assumed an alias. He even resumed teaching in a neighboring state by somehow flying under the radar of a criminal background check. He lasted only a few months, since he soon showed evidence of an anger management problem with his supervisors. But the fact that he was allowed to teach school again, despite his felony convictions, should give all Americans cause for concern.

A shocking case regarding incarceration of the mentally ill was the death of Timothy Souders. Timothy suffered from bipolar disorder, got into trouble and went to jail. His tortuous death was videotaped. Only 21 years old, Tim was in solitary confinement, serving a three -to -five year sentence at the Southern Michigan Correctional Center. CBS News correspondent Scott Pelley brought Souder's plight to the public on February 11, 2007 on CBS TV's *60 Minutes.* Although it was determined he needed psychiatric care, he was chained down. He died of dehydration within a four -day span.

Fact 5:

New York's Law for Assisted Outpatient Treatment (AOT) is referred to as Kendra's Law. The outcome study after the first five years of implementation was shown to "drastically reduce hospitalization, homelessness, arrest, and incarceration among the people with severe psychiatric disorders in the program, while at the same time increasing their adherence to treatment and overall quality of life." (Briefing Paper, OMH, 2005).

* * *

Other states might consider Kendra's Law and the commendable results of providing court-ordered and supervised Assisted Outpatient Treatment (AOT) over the first five years of implementation. Kendra's Law helps the mentally ill who need it most, reduces the profound consequences from lack of treatment and reduces costs for the most expensive services. According to the Briefing Paper, March 30, 2005 from the final report cited above, Kendra's Law reduces harmful behavior, improves treatment compliance, and is highly endorsed by the majority of the recipients. It commits the system to the patient, not only the patient to the system.

Critics of Kendra's Law tend to see court-ordered AOT as a failure of the mental health system. "We view multiple hospitalizations, imprisonment, homelessness and death as system failures, not the level of care that now has significant track record of reducing such failures, which is Assisted Outpatient Treatment," says Ione Christian, President of NAMI in New York State. For an explanation of Kendra's Law go to http://www.omh.state.ny.us/omhweb/Kendra_web/Ksummary.htm.

Fact 6:
Congressional attempts at gun control in this country have not succeeded.

* * *

This history would be a paper unto itself. The National Firearms Act in 1934 and the Safe Streets and Crime Control Act of 1968 did not stop the problem of guns getting into the wrong hands. And despite the national Gun Control Act of 1968, many people suffering from mental illness still purchase guns. This Act intended to stop the sale of guns to people suffering from an incapacitating mental illness, but as many of us have seen, it hasn't been effective in prohibiting the sale of weapons.

As of November 30, 2007, thirty-two states have submitted names to the mental-health database, while the federal government lacked the power to force the other 18 to do so. On January 8, 2008, President Bush signed legislation aimed at preventing the seriously mentally ill from purchasing guns by tightening checks on them. Although the bill had been introduced in 2002 after a shooting in a church, it gained momentum with the Virginia Tech massacre in April 2007. Unfortunately, Seung-Hui Cho had been able to pass a background check and buy two guns even though a Virginia court had found him mentally ill. From all indications Cho didn't receive the court-ordered outpatient treatment he was supposed to receive, nor had his court order been submitted to the federal database.

Since then, Representative Bobby Rush (D-IL) sponsored H.R. 45-Blair Holt's Firearm Licensing and Record of Sale Act of 2009. This bill amends the Brady Handgun Violence Prevention Act. It attempts to prohibit unlicensed gun ownership through a nation-wide system mandating gun owners to apply for five-year licenses to own firearms. It is considered a fringe bill with no cosponsors and little chance of being voted into law. (www.opencongress.org/bill/111-h45/show, retrieved on 5/21/11.).

Fact 7:

Progress in mental health laws is being made slowly around the United States.

* * *

One example is Illinois' new Public Act 95-602 (2007), effective June 1, 2008. It was introduced as Senate Bill 234 and according to the Treatment Advocacy Center (2008) SB 234 it expands the scope the state's commitment criteria, which formerly required that a person with a severe mental illness be *expected to inflict serious physical harm* in the near future before a court can authorize involuntary treatment. The new criteria permits court-ordered treatment for individuals who, while not presenting a demonstrable threat of immediate physical harm to themselves or others, are clearly in need of psychiatric care and whose condition is likely to create a risk of serious harm to the person or others absent treatment.

In the 1960s and 1970s, state laws were reformed to require a court finding of "immediate dangerousness to the person or to others" in order to involuntarily treat severe mental illness, such as schizophrenia and manic depression. Despite the hopes of sincere reformers, many of the most seriously ill went without treatment and the consequences were indeed dire. The Treatment Advocacy Center (2008) states:

In 1999, the Department of Justice reported that as much as 16 percent of the population of state jails and prisons, more than 260,000 individuals, suffer from severe mental illnesses.

At least 150,000 to 200,000 people, or one-third of the nation's homeless population, suffer from severe mental illnesses.

About 5,000 people suffering from schizophrenia or bipolar illness commit suicide each year.

Fortunately, about half of the states have been actively reforming their standards during the last twenty years. Factors considered in these laws include "deteriorating condition, need for treatment, inability to make informed treatment decisions, likelihood of becoming dangerous absent treatment, and the capability of independent functioning." So far, none of these state laws have been found to be unconstitutional. The highest courts of Washington (1986), Wisconsin (2002) and New York (2004) have all found these reforms to be constitutional (Treatment Advocacy Center, 2008).

Mental illness and substance abuse problems are generally treated separately in the United States. Often funding and the credentials of the treatment professionals promote that separation. Mental illness does not equate to violence. The general public perception of mental illness includes much stigma and fear of violence. A relatively new study sheds light on this belief.

In 2001-2002, an original survey involving 43,000 face-to-face interviews with a representative sample of American adults was analyzed by researchers from the National Epidemiologic Survey on Alcohol and Related Conditions. Three years later, over 34,000 of the original interview sample were questioned again.

Jillian Duchinowski and Carla K. Johnson summarized some of the survey's findings in their article entitled Violence Produces Violence—Study: Mental Illness Doesn't Trigger Behavior:

There were 3,089 people deemed to have severe mental illness—schizophrenia, bipolar disorder and major depression— but no history of either violence or substance abuse. They reported very few violent acts, about 50, between interviews.

But when mental illness was combined with a history of violence and a history of substance abuse (involving 1,600 people), the risk of future violence increased by a factor of 10.

To complicate matters, symptoms of mental disorders are not static over time. According to Dr. Ken Duckworth, NAMI's current medical director:

People present different symptoms at different times in their lives, and that's important. If you look at someone living with bipolar disorder when they're well and they can't articulate a prior episode, it could be easy for a clinician to underestimate how ill they were— or are. Looking at the whole person's life is crucial to getting a good diagnosis. Then, diagnosis is a springboard to getting the right treatment. Doctors need to use that information to figure out what would be the best set of interventions to move their patients' lives forward (Reyers,2010).

It cannot be emphasized enough that collaboration with families, mental health professionals and law enforcement agencies are essential, without waiting for actual and immediate physical danger. I have hope that reforms will continue to address the needs of the mentally ill. One hopeful note occurred on July 28 2010, when Governor Pat Quinn of Illinois signed Senate Bill 851 into law. Marriage and family therapists are now included as providers who can sign an emergency petition admitting individuals to a mental health facility. (September/October, 2010) *Family Therapy Magazine,* Alexandria, VA, AAMFT, Inc.

Our nation mourned when Congresswoman Gabrielle Giffords was shot in Tucson by Jared Lee Loughner, age 22, on January 8, 2011. Twelve others were shot and six people died. Jared had been demonstrating unusual behavior prior to her shooting. But again, a tragedy occurred before he was identified as someone in need of serious help for untreated symptoms of a mental illness. (www.

nytimes.com/2011/01/09/us/politics, retrieved on 11/17/11.). The media emphasized a great need for bipartisan civility after the tragedy. There is no doubt we are in need of that. But it minimized the greater issue which is dealing with untreated symptoms of a mental disorder.

On October 5, 2011 The Arizona Department of Health Services opened a new secure facility at the Arizona State Hospital for treatment of the mentally ill. An article in *The Arizona Republic* on October 6, 2011 announced that the $32.2 million hospital has 120 beds and will serve patients who have been found to be "guilty but insane" in the court system. It also includes therapy centers. It will provide better care for patients and more security for staff than the former facility. It is a small, but significant step forward.

I envision a day when, with the help of ongoing research, we are able to reduce the scourge of mental illness and the tremendous cost to individuals, families and communities. Bipolar disorder ranks the highest in expense as a behavioral health care diagnosis. It costs over twice as much for each afflicted individual as depression. And every one dollar spent for those patients in outpatient treatment costs one dollar and eighty cents for inpatient care. (www.cdc.gov/mental).

In the meantime, we can encourage a reduction in the stigma of mental illness with our own attitudes. We can contact our legislators to encourage more enlightened mental health laws and access to treatment for those who are afflicted. Early interventions, brief stabilization, medication and better coordination of care would all be steps on this journey. I would love to see more specialized mental health courts and multi-disciplinary crisis intervention teams. The criminal-justice system cannot function in the role of a mental-health provider. We can contribute to medical research aimed at genetic studies. We can let others know about the support and advocacy offered by NAMI across the country for patients and family members who want help. Memoirs such as mine may shed light on problems by trying to put a family's face on numbing statistics. We continue to need solid research to support these anecdotal records.

REFERENCE LIST

Bipolar Disorder Today, NIMH, (n.d.) Retrieved November 22, 2010 from www.mental-health-today.com/bp.

Boszormenyi-Nagy, Ivan and Spark, Geraldine M. (1984) *Invisible Loyalties*. New York: Brunner/Mazel, pp. 369- 370.

Center for Disease Control. Retrieved January 23, 2012 from www.cdc.gov.mental.health.

Duchnowski, Jillian and Johnson, Carla K. (2009) Violence Produces Violence— Study: Mental Illness Doesn't Trigger Behavior. The Associated Press. Retrieved 2/3/2009, from www.nwherald.com.

An Explanation of Kendra's Law. New York State, Office of Mental Health, November 1999.Revised May 2006. Retrieved December 30, 2007 from www.omh.state.ny.us.

Faherty, John. (2011, October 6). State hospital opens facility for patients in court system. *The Arizona Republic*, p. B2.

Family Therapy Magazine. Division Advocacy. (September/October, 2010) AAMFT, Inc., p. 6.

Federal law tightens checks on gun buyers. (2008, January 9). *The Arizona Republic*, A1.

Gun Control Act of 1968. Retrieved September 29, 2011 from www.usgov.info.about.com.

H.R. 45-Blair Holt's Firearm Licensing and Record of Sale Act of 2009, retrieved on 5/21/11 from www.opencongress.org.

Kimball, Angela. (2007) Make NAMI's Voice Heard in Election 2008. *NAMI Advocate*, Fall 2007, 11.

Lacey, Marc and Herszenhorn, David M. (2011, January 9). New York Times, In Attack's Wake, Political Repercussions. Retrieved November 17, 2011 from www.nytimes.com/2011/01/09/us/politics.

National Institute of Mental Health, *The Numbers Count: Mental Disorders in America*, 2006 (rev). Retrieved May 13, 2008 from www.nimh.nih.gov.

November Coalition, *The Death of Timothy Souders. Retrieved September 10, 2007 from* www.november.org.

N.Y. State Office of Mental Health (March 2005). Kendra's Law: Final report of the status of assisted outpatient treatment. Briefing paper (March 30, 2005) [Electronic version.] New York: Office of Mental Health.

Reinhart, Mary K. (2011, May 22). The issue: The number of Arizonans who live with a diagnosable mental illness. *The Arizona Republic*, p. B2.

Reyers, Courtney. (Fall 2010). What Are They Thinking? Research, Diagnosis and Mental Illness. *NAMI Advocate*, Vol. 8, No. 3, p.13.

Torrey, E. Fuller, M.D., Kennard, Sheriff Aaron D., Eslinger, Sheriff Don, Lamb, Richard, M.D., and Pavle, James, Treatment Advocacy Center and the National Sheriff's Association. *More Mentally Ill Persons are in Jails and Prisons than Hospitals*, May 18, 2010. Retrieved on November 23, 2011 from www.treatmentadvocacycenter.org .

Treatment Advocacy Center, Analysis of SB234. (n.d.) Retrieved May 11, 2008 from www.treatmentandadvocacycenter.org.

Vergakis, Brock and Jordan, Lara Jakes. (2007, November 30). Banned gun-buyers list grows. *The Arizona Republic*, p. A6.

Xplore, Inc.,   BrainyQuote™.   Created   2001.   http://www.brainyquote.com/quotes/authors/aeschylus.html (Accessed 30 December 2008)

Made in the USA
Charleston, SC
01 November 2013